THE ART
OF
BARTER

THE ART
OF
BARTER

HOW TO TRADE FOR ALMOST ANYTHING

KAREN S. HOFFMAN
AND
SHERA D. DALIN

Skyhorse P

Skyhorse Publishing books may be purchased in bulk at special discounts for sales promotion, corporate gifts, fund-raising, or educational purposes. Special editions can also be created to specifications. For details, contact the Special Sales Department, Skyhorse Publishing, 555 Eighth Avenue, Suite 903, New York, NY 10018 or info@skyhorsepublishing.com.

www.skyhorsepublishing.com

10 9 8 7 6 5 4 3 2 1

Library of Congress Cataloging-in-Publication Data

Hoffman, Karen S.
    The art of barter: how to trade for almost anything / Karen S. Hoffman and Shera D. Dalin.
        p. cm.
    ISBN 978-1-60239-953-2 (pbk. : alk. paper)
    1. Barter. I. Dalin, Shera D. II. Title.
    HF1019.H64 2010
    332'.54--dc22

                                                2010008007

Printed in the United States of America

To my awesome husband, Rick: Can you believe after all these years, I *still* look forward to being with you? And to my grown children—Mitzi, Jaime, Joe, and my "bonus" daughter, Carol—I'm so blessed to be your mom. Much love to my adorable grandkids, Jessica and Cody, and my "babies," Melia, Ava, and Danielle. Life is so much sweeter because of all of you!

—Karen S. Hoffman

For my sweet angel Mereya and my dear, supportive husband, Jorge, who always believes in me. Thank you for making my life rich with joy, adventure, and laughter.

—Shera D. Dalin

CONTENTS

ACKNOWLEDGMENTS

There are so many people who have impacted this book and my life. Some people I will mention have passed on, but they absolutely affected my life in such positive ways. My apologies for anyone I've forgotten to mention here; you are still in my heart.

Thanks so much to our agent, Krista Goering, for believing in Shera Dalin and me. Thanks to our editor, Ann Treistman, from Skyhorse Publishing—what a joy you have been to work with!

Without Michael Gershman (author of *Smarter Barter*), Phil Donahue (yes, the former TV talk show host), and Stuart Burstein (owner of the local Barter System International franchise), I would never have discovered retail barter. Thank you, all.

To my hundreds and hundreds of very cool clients, thank you for sharing the journey of learning together about the benefits of barter and creative ways to use it. My special thanks to clients who were with me from the beginning of my own barter company in the late '80s: Steve Bunyard, who gifted me with my single largest deal—a million-dollar transaction; Joe Eisenberg, who rescued me when I realized that this million-dollar transaction needed warehousing; Marty Daly, another big thinker who saw the potential that barter has yet to reach here in the United States; Steve and Cindy Tornatore, who have always treated their barter clients as wonderfully as they treated their cash customers. It was rewarding to serve you, and I count you not only as clients but as friends.

My deepest thanks to the three guys who helped me keep my barter spirits up and reenergized me when I was low: Bob Meyer, the publisher of *Barter News* magazine; Gary Monkman, a dear friend and an exchange owner in Waukegan, Illinois; and Paul St. Martin with the Allan Hackel Organization. Thanks for your time and our talks.

To some brilliant barter and business minds and those who gave so much to the International Reciprocal Trade Association and to me: Alan Elkin, Allan Hackel, Steve Goldbloom (thanks for your belief in me), Scott Whittmer (wow; as a board member, you gave and gave!), Susan Groenwald, Mary Ellen Rosinski, Lois Dale (the Queen of Barter), Reiner Husemann, Paul Suplizio, and Pascal Alexandre. Working with and learning from all of you was an honor.

To Bruce Kamm—I love your "possibility" mind and how you saw such big things for the barter industry. Paul and Collette McConville—what awesome friends, what caring hearts. Mike Baer, wherever you are, thanks for your belief in me as well and for listening to my many ideas and running with them. Dawn Kerns and Larry Knaus, thanks for tolerating me as your boss for many years. Richard Harris, when we were not annoying each other, our passion for barter and making deals united us. I give thanks to the following people who, in addition to the service they have given to the barter industry, helped me research this book: again, Bob Meyer, Terry and Lee Brandfass, David Wallach, Harold Rice, Mauyra Lane, John Moore, and Alexandra Hart. Thank you, thank you!

Thanks also to so many people who contributed their time, knowledge, and wisdom to this book: Zeo Solomon and Amir Razmara, Debbie Bozsa, Dawn Maturen, all the folks at Active International, Maurya Lane for her tremendous sense of humor and incredible patience at answering unending questions, and the many other experts who helped in their own ways.

For the many "wings" beneath my sails, believing in me, helping me, in all my endeavors, I thank Linda Binns, Laura Schacht, Angela Lieb, Laura Herring, Sandy Brickey, Sue Schneider, Judy Ryan, Mary Kay Sheets, Julie Hood, Jackie Cook, Donna Gamache, Suzi Tozer, Tessa Greenspan, Kelly Alcorn, Karen Garcia, and so many more; my ESPW (Encouraging, Supporting Promoting Women) family; my eWomen Network family; and my Uncle Marty. I am truly blessed beyond belief.

Lastly, Shera Dalin; what a joy it's been to collaborate and work on this book together. The flow was fantastic. You are brilliant, and you made this project so much fun! I adore you!

INTRODUCTION

Although barter is the oldest form of transaction in the world, we are always amazed at how often people are startled by the idea of using barter in their everyday lives. Our culture is so cash-focused that for all but an inventive few, most of us have forgotten this age-old system of exchange that much of the developing world still employs. However, as you'll see in the following pages, barter is very much alive and well in the twenty-first century. Plenty of people—plumbers, secretaries, writers, hairstylists, moms, stockbrokers, and so on—trade their skills for goods and services they need or simply want. And for those who use barter, the results are dramatic. They save money, create new relationships, stabilize family finances, pay off and avoid debt, acquire luxuries, and improve the overall well-being of their families, just by being creative thinkers.

Our goal in writing this book is to expand possibilities. We will explain how you can use barter in your daily life to acquire the things you want and need without having to use cash (or at least not as much of it). We'll explain how barter works and what doesn't work. We'll share stories with you from our own varied trading experiences, and we'll have lots of examples of regular people like you who use barter for the things they don't want to spend cash on (or don't have cash for). You'll learn about people who traded for everything from haircuts to houses, blouses to boats, and cats to cars. The wonderful thing about barter is that you leave a world limited by cash and enter the universe of unlimited possibility and creativity. All you have to do is put some effort and imagination into it.

Barter is especially helpful if your circumstances have temporarily diminished your cash flow. People who have been laid off, had their hours cut, or are just getting into the workforce should absolutely consider barter as a way to offset cash expenses and help with obtaining products and services they need while they job hunt or wait for their company's finances to improve. When you barter your time and talents, you also relieve the stress from financial hardships and provide income that can lift your spirits so you can keep going. The products and services you barter can also help you stay out of debt as you reconfigure your life. It also shows you another way of managing the world and that your worth isn't connected to just a paycheck. Barter could, in fact, solve your money problems, and at the very least, it can certainly help.

Beyond finances, we are excited about barter's potential—really, *your* potential—to change your world into a more engaged, involved, and caring place. Just like the old-fashioned barn raising where all the neighbors came to help one farmer erect his barn, barter helps you build a better, bigger

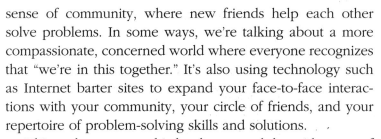

sense of community, where new friends help each other solve problems. In some ways, we're talking about a more compassionate, concerned world where everyone recognizes that "we're in this together." It's also using technology such as Internet barter sites to expand your face-to-face interactions with your community, your circle of friends, and your repertoire of problem-solving skills and solutions.

Ultimately, we want this book to reveal the wide array of possibilities that barter can bring into your life and the joys that will come with them.

To bountiful bartering!

Karen S. Hoffman
Shera D. Dalin

CHAPTER 1

WHAT BARTER CAN DO FOR YOU

If you want to teach people a new way of thinking, don't bother trying to teach them. Instead, give them a tool, the use of which will lead to new ways of thinking.

—Buckminster Fuller

In 1972, high school sweethearts Karen and Rick Hoffman had been married only a few months and were living in Rick's mom's basement apartment. The couple really wanted to buy a house, but, like a lot of newlyweds, they had little money and no prospects for getting enough for a down payment on a house anytime soon. Karen, who was only eighteen at the time, began calling real estate companies to ask if there were any rental homes available.

Each agent responded in nearly the same way: Little or no rental property was available, but would she like to buy a house?

Karen was frustrated by the lack of homes for rent, but she began paying attention to how the agents discussed the properties they had for sale. Always an acute listener, she began piecing together tidbits of information that the agents dropped. One talked about the requirements of getting a home loan through the Federal Housing Administration (FHA), but the couple would have to come up with closing costs, which they didn't have. Another discussed asking a seller to pay closing costs because he was "highly motivated."

Hmmm, thought Karen. *There's more to this story than just buying a home. If I can just put these pieces together, there may be room for negotiation.*

Excited and nervous, Karen began looking at prospective houses, but nothing she saw fit their tiny budget—as well as Rick's race car and gear and their dogs, Sam and Spooky. Karen gave up on working with an agent to find a home. Instead, she and Rick decided to make their own destiny. They drove through neighborhoods in the area where they'd grown up—first hers, then his—looking for houses for rent or homes that looked vacant. On their first trip out, they found nothing. But on only their second trip, they found a vacant but enticing small ranch for sale on a cul-de-sac. It had a garage that would hold Rick's race car and a fenced yard that would be perfect for the dogs. Like a good omen, it was on a street named Rickey. Although they didn't want to get their hopes up too much, it certainly seemed to be exactly what they were looking for.

They called the agent representing the home owner and discovered that the owner lived out of state and was tired of dealing with renters, repairs, and hassles. While the little fifteen-year-old ranch was structurally sound, its insides were a mess. There was psychedelic paint covering the walls, two-by-fours painted black and nailed to the living room walls as "decor," hardwood floors with significant damage, a sidewalk that needed new cement, and minor work that needed to be done to the exterior. The seller was willing to go through FHA to sell her home but didn't want to invest the money, and she lived too far away to handle all the repairs that would make the home eligible for an FHA loan.

The deal seemed doomed before they could even get started, but, Karen, ever the creative thinker, began to ponder other ways to make it happen.

"What if we offered to make all the repairs that were needed in exchange for living in the house without paying rent?" Karen proposed to Rick. Since Rick was quite a handyman (and would later become a contractor), he loved the idea.

They made their proposal to the seller's real estate agent, and the home owner agreed. In the meantime, they worked to save the few hundred dollars they needed for their down payment while rehabbing the home. They poured all of their time and energy into hammering, patching, wallpapering, and laying flooring, and within six months, they had saved enough to make the down payment and were ready to close. As agreed, the seller paid the closing costs. That and Rick's job enabled them to qualify for that FHA loan. Because of Karen's innovative idea, the young couple had their first home in a short time and with little money.

In fact, having a house so early in their marriage allowed the Hoffmans to build up $10,000 in equity that would serve to help them buy a larger home when Karen was only twenty-one and Rick was twenty-two. The equity in that home accrued and allowed them to purchase larger houses as their family grew and needed more space. Eventually, the couple was able to build their dream home, again, using the equity from their previous houses as well as cash they had saved from the many other trades they had made for items they wanted or needed.

Barter became a powerful force in the life of Karen and her family from that point forward.

SO WHAT CAN BARTER DO FOR YOU?

Probably more than you imagine. All you'll need is your imagination and a little help from this book to put barter to use in your life. It also helps to have a willingness to put aside the beliefs that all of us have grown up with: that you have to save money, make money, or borrow money to buy the things you want. This is probably the hardest thing for all of us to learn. Stop before whipping out a wallet, a checkbook, or a debit or credit card and ponder, Is there another way I can get what I need or want?

When you embrace bartering, you bring a host of benefits into your life that you hadn't considered before. The A-number-one benefit you reap from barter is saving cash. If you can barter your services for something you would normally pay for, you have clearly freed your cash for something that you can't get through barter.

Trading can save you time. If you're like us, you would rather visit the dentist than have to clean house. So bartering for housecleaning is a mighty fine way to avoid doing a chore you dislike and free up your time to do something you do like, perhaps by keeping the books for your housecleaning company or babysitting for the owner's children. Doesn't spending more time doing what you love to do rather than trudging through something you hate to do sound like a far more appealing way to live your life?

If you're concerned about the environment, barter is a great way to recycle. Instead of dumping your stuff into the trash stream, barter it to keep it out of our growing landfills and productive for someone who really needs it.

Another pleasantly unexpected benefit to barter is how it strengthens friendships and builds your sense of community in ways you wouldn't have anticipated. Shera trades her writing and marketing skills with a concierge doctor, who, in turn, cares for Shera's family. In a cash-only system, Shera's family would never have considered paying $3,000 a year on top of insurance for a doctor's care. But in this case, the doctor makes house calls and is available by cell phone, 24/7. Since traditional doctors don't usually provide their personal cell-phone numbers or drop by the house to check on your child's rash, Shera is delighted to be able to use her talents to obtain such a wonderfully luxurious commodity that would have been otherwise out of reach. Her husband, a busy executive, loves having a concierge doctor because he doesn't have to wait in her office and saves hours in his time-crunched day. But beyond the benefits of having such great care, Shera has become friends with her doctor in a way that she has never been able to with any other medical professional. Because she and her doctor meet for lunch, chat about their families, and, oh yeah, get a little work done in the process, they have established a friendship that not only helps both of them do better work for each other but also broadens their base of friends and their sense of community.

Building a sense of community through barter happens in many other ways. Working moms and dads might appreciate the system that two families in St. Louis created. These two couples, each with young children, agreed to host dinner for the other couple once a week. During those dinners, the couples were able to taste recipes that were new to them, leave behind the pressure of making dinner that night, hang out with their friends, share a glass or two of wine, and let their kids romp with each other in a safe environment.

"We figure it's a night of entertainment since the adults get to talk and the kids get to run around together, and at least one family gets a break from making a weeknight meal," explains mom Valerie Hahn.

Some people have used barter to create babysitting co-ops that not only saved them hundreds of dollars on sitters but also built a sense of community and lifelong friendships and allowed them to live richer lives because they weren't tied to the dollar.

In a cash transaction, you write a check or swipe your credit card and then consume your goods or service as just another customer. But the very nature of barter makes it more personal and builds friendships that can last beyond the length of the barter arrangement. Simply setting up the deal ensures that you are going to have a much more interactive relationship than a cash sale. And that relationship often grows, bringing more barter opportunities your way. When your trading partner is happy with the transaction, he or she is more likely to refer other barter deals your way, assuming you've got the goods or capacity to meet the demand. If you want repeat trades or referrals, treat people right. Karen traded her coaching services with a chiropractor and was so delighted with the treatment she received that she referred the chiropractor to five friends who then became paying patients of the chiropractor, amounting to thousands of dollars of revenue.

When you don't swipe that credit card to get what you need, you've just taken a bit of pressure off your family's finances and left room on your credit line that you may need for other purchases. Since cash and, more than ever before, credit are scarce, avoiding the need to access a credit line will also help you keep your credit score high or improve it over time. If your credit cards are maxed out, barter opens up a whole world of goods and services that were simply unavailable to you via plastic or the often-elusive bank loan.

The psychological impact that barter has on you and your family can be tremendously positive. Depression occurs and self-esteem drops when you cannot provide for those you love. So if you are struggling with debt, have lost your job, or just need more money, barter can help you handle those pressures by providing other avenues of getting what you want or need. If you can barter for child care, you've taken a huge stressor off your list of worries. Your children will be able to sense when you are less stressed and more relaxed on a daily basis. If you're feeling less pressure, you'll be in a better frame of mind and more likely to interact with your kids in a positive way. Less stress means less yelling and less tension and more happiness all around. You can't measure the immense value of a healthier, happier home life.

But what if it's not a product or service that you need? Perhaps what you're really hunting for is education; barter can help there too. There are universities, community colleges, and trade schools that barter from time to time. Perhaps you can work in office administration, libraries, or classrooms; write newsletters; cater; and so on in trade for your tuition.

Perhaps traditional education may not be exactly what you're looking for. What if you've lost a job and need to get experience in a new industry? You could apply to be an intern, but then you'd be competing with the entire field of college kids who are seeking the same internships. (Plus you might feel a tad awkward being an intern if you've got more salt than pepper in your hair.) Karen's uncle Don gave us a lesson in how to barter time for education.

Don was between jobs and really had the urge to get into the radio business. He was intrigued by it and thought it would be fun, as well as enable him to earn a living. So he visited a radio station he liked and applied for a job. He was turned down. He applied again and was turned down. Determined to work for the station, he offered to be an unpaid salesman for two weeks, so he could learn the ropes. They said yes. For two weeks, Don worked his tail off learning the radio sales game. At the end of that time, he was offered a paying job where none had been available before. Don bartered his way into an excellent, hands-on education and a paying job. Better still, within about five years, Don had advanced at the station to become its general manager. The guy who had bartered his time was now running the show. Even if he had never been hired at that station, Don still would have learned valuable sales skills that he could apply at another station or in a related field.

Don is a perfect example of someone who was unemployed and used barter—in the sense of trading time for opportunities—to reinvent himself. Most people frantically begin job hunting when they get a pink slip, which is a perfectly understandable reaction. But when the economy is in recession or jobs are simply hard to find in your field, barter is an option that can open new doors for you. If you lose your secretarial job but have secretly yearned to open your own restaurant, barter can help you get started. Maybe you've never worked in a restaurant and have no idea where to begin. No problem. Barter your time like Don did and get the experience you need, along with the inside tips, tricks, and strategies of running a restaurant, all for the cost of your time. Plus, you won't jeopardize your unemployment insurance because you'll be working for free while you learn. We want you to begin to view your time as a valuable asset that is worth using in order to receive something equally valuable in exchange.

Maybe what you really want is time with a career counselor or outplacement specialist to help you fine-tune your résumé or interviewing skills. Or possibly you just need help figuring out what your next career should be. Barter can help you access those services without having to deplete your dwindling cash reserves. Perhaps a personal Web site with a portfolio or other reference material is what you lack; trading your skills with a webmaster could solve that problem without cash changing hands. You get a professionally designed Web site to show off your work, and the webmaster gets an advocate in you, another site to add to his or her portfolio, and a bit of advertising at the bottom of your home page.

Chances are also good that you've got skills from your downsized job that you can trade for what you need. While cash is still king, you can ease your need for hard currency by trading your carpenter services (or whatever your talent is) for, say, restaurant gift certificates for a few free meals at the place you helped remodel. Maybe you used to have a job as a buyer or procurement clerk; have you thought about helping a small business get the best deals on their raw materials with your top-notch bargaining skills? If you're a tech guru, you can trade your information technology savvy for child care that will give you free time to job hunt. What about trading your technology skills for upgrades on the technology you need but can't afford?

Another area that is always ripe for barter is marketing. Your marketing skills can help a graphic designer who is redoing a restaurant's menu or signage. A public relations specialist can help promote nearly any business. Any talent that is marketing related holds special appeal to business owners, who will be apt to trade services with you. Clearly, the potential is enormous, limited only by your imagination and willingness to give it a go.

Barter isn't just about acquiring stuff; it can also be about getting rid of stuff, too—namely, all of those items currently cluttering up your basement, attic, shed, barn, closets, trunk, space under the beds, and storage unit. (This also means saving on storage fees for the unit once you empty it out.) By offering to barter your excess furniture, bikes, kids' clothes, and maybe even that dusty treadmill—we know you had good intentions, but just think about how much guilt you'll be free of once you pass it on to someone who will actually use it—you free up space for the great new items you'll get and actually use. Maybe you'll trade those items for a service like dry cleaning so that you can avoid re cluttering the garage. Best of all, you'll be keeping your unwanted junk out of a landfill and getting it back into use by someone who truly wants it. Voilà! You've become a trader and an environmentalist. Didn't know you had it in you, huh?

So now that you and the kids have traded all those old clothes from your now-clean and organized closets for newer ones, how about a vacation, compliments of barter? Many savvy folks who don't have enough disposable income to afford a cruise or time at a fancy resort still get to have fabulous vacations because they barter for them. Perhaps you can trade your handyman skills for the cruise or your housecleaning labor for the resort stay. The trick on this sort of luxury-item barter is that you'll almost certainly have to find someone on the inside of the vacation provider who can help you make a direct trade happen. Bartering directly with a cruise line, airline, or resort is difficult, generally speaking, although not impossible. However, a commercial barter exchange, which is a for-profit company that brokers trades and handles all the accounting for you, will give you options on other vacations that the most in-demand spots won't allow. Hotels, bed-and-breakfast inns, or smaller, family-owned resorts will be trading options on an exchange. With an exchange-based trade, you will get a tremendous amount of flexibility, a faster conclusion to the transaction, and access to vacation options you wouldn't have had otherwise.

If you prefer a less-programmed vacation, there are options for swapping homes—even with families who live overseas.

There are Web sites such as HomeExchange.com that connect people who want to swap their homes with others in locations all over the world. (Read more about this in chapter 6, and find a list of barter Web sites in the Resources section.) Here's your chance to pack your luggage for a vacation in Paris or San Diego or wherever—for no cash.

Perhaps you're the type of person who has a big heart but a small wallet. You'd like to give more to your favorite cause or charity, but you just don't have the disposable income to do it. We automatically assume that we must spend money to support the charitable causes we love. Money doesn't always have to be the solution. Instead of writing a check, you can use barter as a creative avenue to help a cause. How about bartering your services or time? Find the company that produces what your charity needs and offer your services or goods to that company in exchange for a donation of what your charitable cause needs. It's not only a win for your charity; it also gives the company supplying the wish-list item an opportunity to support a good cause and gain a bit of public goodwill for doing so.

An organization that Shera belongs to was holding a trivia night fund-raiser and used barter to lower the costs that the trivia master charged. Members of the organization used their personal Twitter accounts to send out promotional "tweets" about the trivia master working with the organization. In exchange for those tweets and some other promotional efforts, the trivia master lowered his costs by about 20 percent. He got great publicity, and the organization saved money, which could then be used for scholarships. Everybody won. (Check out chapter 8 to learn more about charitable giving and barter.)

Maybe your desires lean more toward the for-profit world. Budding entrepreneurs can use barter to save money on business start-up costs, which can often be dream-killing obstacles. We know many entrepreneurs who have used their

skills not only to save money on starting their businesses but also to attract new customers at the same time. When Shera first started her writing business, Karen introduced her to a women's entrepreneur organization that needed public relations help. Shera traded her PR and press release writing talents for membership in this influential businesswomen's networking organization. That membership gave Shera access to a large group of women entrepreneurs that she would have been hard-pressed to meet and interact with otherwise. Barter is a powerful tool in the entrepreneur's tool kit, and it is one that is too often overlooked.

THE BOTTOM LINE

Obviously we aren't saying you will be able to get everything you want through barter—at least not immediately. It's true that some items, particularly those that are in high demand or in short supply, may not be available for barter. Temporarily. When the demand drops or the supply goes up, the barter option returns to the table. Patience is an absolute necessity when you barter.

What it all boils down to is that barter opens up an entire realm of possibilities and ideas that you never considered before. Barter is the tool that helps to create possibilities in your head and your heart. Our hope is that you, instead of reciting mantras like "I can't afford it" or "We shouldn't spend our money on that," start saying, "Why is it so easy for me to barter for what I want and need?" Indeed, we hope this will become your affirmation.

Whether you barter to help your family, yourself, or a friend, bartering is a tool that can affect you emotionally, physically, and financially. Trading can make you a more creative problem solver, more self-reliant, and more hopeful. This is especially true if you are dealing with a large debt load, underemployed, or unemployed. The sense of defeat and despair that arises in those situations for most people can yield to a new sense of opportunity, broader horizons, and optimism for the future—a future less needful of cash.

GREAT TRADE!

Jacqueline Freeman wins our award for Amazing Trader, not only for sheer volume but also for inventiveness. Jacqueline and her husband, Joseph, are organic farmers at Friendly Haven Rise Farm in Venersborg, Washington (population 3,000). Jacqueline admits that she's got an advantage because she lives in a small town, where bartering is easier. She's also got a leg up because she's a farmer, and farmers are barterers by nature and tradition. But she insists that barter isn't just for country folks. When she was an urbanite living in Seattle, she once provided an elderly woman with physical therapy in exchange for home-baked treats. The patient desperately needed the treatment but couldn't afford it, and Medicare reimbursed only a small fraction of the cost; in addition, the patient was too proud to accept charity despite her pain. By bartering, both women came out winners. Jacqueline was thrilled to have home-baked goodies in exchange for helping someone in need to heal; the patient got the treatment she needed with her pride and dignity intact and without going broke.

Jacqueline has also traded a seat in the beekeeping classes she teaches for pepperoni venison and homemade preserves. One woman attended the class in exchange for home-baked organic fruit pies. Jacqueline has bartered a beehive for Cutco knives; half a butchered cow for using a neighbor's pasture and barn for a year and haying his field; dental fillings for physical therapy; two young calves for a butchered hog, cut up and ready to go into her freezer; her artistic ability creating menus for free meals (very helpful when she was a broke twenty-something); a stay on her farm for a radio host and her husband in exchange for being featured on their show

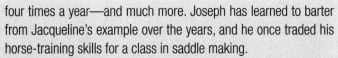

four times a year—and much more. Joseph has learned to barter from Jacqueline's example over the years, and he once traded his horse-training skills for a class in saddle making.

"Anything that improves my life is a good trade," Jacqueline says, even when the trade is a bit lopsided in the other person's favor.

The key is to be open to barter opportunities and listen carefully when people talk about what they need in life. Chances to barter are everywhere if you start looking for them, even just casually, she says. That's how she runs across most of her trades, and she's sure you can do the same, if you're open.

TRADING TIP

Start keeping your ears and eyes open for chances to barter. Listen to what people say they lack or need. Once you become more attuned to the opportunities to make trades, more of them will come your way. Take a chance and ask if they want to trade!

CHAPTER 2

THE BARTER LURKING AROUND YOUR HOUSE

*Ideas create possibilities. Possibilities offer hope.
Create some!*

—Karen S. Hoffman

There are barter opportunities hiding all around your home. They are under the bed, lounging in your attic, lurking in your basement, sneaking around your garage. Here you were, living in your humble abode all this time, and you had no idea. Don't blame yourself. You're not the only one who doesn't know about all that wealth hiding in plain sight. Even the best traders forget about the stuff they have that could be bartered. So let's take a peek inside those boxes in the basement and the dark corners of your closet to see what's hanging out in there that could save you some cash.

TURNING GOODS INTO GOODIES

We'll start with the easy stuff. You'll need your favorite notepad, writing utensil, and maybe a digital camera if you have one. Pick a room in your home. Instead of looking at the things you usually focus on in this room, notice the items that you rarely pay attention to. What things are cluttering the space? Maybe that chair that's become a place to throw your coats—the one that hasn't felt your backside in months, maybe years? It could be your next barter victory. Check under the bed. Chances are there are items stored underneath that you've long forgotten about that need a good home (excluding the dust bunnies). Check the drawers in your bureau, especially those "junk drawers." If you haven't worn, sat on, played with, displayed, or used it in more than year, you won't miss it. Time to prowl through the dark corners of your closet: Are there clothes, coats, boots, purses, hats, or other accessories that could go back into circulation?

Start collecting these items in a central location and writing down what each one is. Include a brief description, including brand names, sizes, or other information that will help you sort through it. If you've got a digital camera, take some shots so you can upload them to barter Web sites when you're ready. A few different angles—including ones that show logos or other identifying information, as well as any flaws—will be helpful. Make the objects look as attractive as possible. In this day of high-end advertising, consumers expect top-notch graphics. Traders will accept lower standards, of course, but we're all human and highly attuned to the onslaught of the product beauty pageant. Fuzzy, dimly lit photos won't help you make any trades.

If there are items you are debating putting up for barter, just put a question mark beside them and see how you feel in a few days or a week. You may decide that they are too precious to part with or, after a bit of time, more like clutter than treasure.

Don't get distracted cleaning or trying on items as you go through the sorting process; you can do that later. Rather, focus your energy on finding, cataloging, describing, and assigning a value to the items you can trade. Besides, it'll be easier to clean when you've transferred all your excess stuff to someone else's home.

Do this same task room by room. Make sure you root through the garage, attic, basement, and other unused areas of your home. Poke around in boxes, shelves that haven't been disturbed for ages, toy chests that haven't been investigated by little hands for several months, and any other neglected container.

Don't take the furniture for granted. Is there a table, desk, chair, chest, or other furnishing that you could refinish so that it fetches a better trade? Would a new covering on a cushion, often an easy repair, make a set of dining chairs more up-to-date and a definite must-have? If you've got a small appliance or electronic device that is beyond your skills to repair or refurbish, don't worry—you've still got a potential trade on hand. Handymen love snapping up those sorts of items to fix and sell for a nice price.

Random objects such as mismatched tools, picture-hanging supplies, spackle, and the like could be lumped together as a fix-it kit. Gather up your unused hair ornaments, extra beauty supplies, and stray costume jewelry and label it "Girl's Dress-Up Kit" or "Makeover Magic Collection." Sometimes a little creative marketing goes a long way. Just make sure you can describe the most attractive or valuable objects in the collection to get traders interested in the whole kit and caboodle. If you've got a spare decorative box or the energy to wrap a plain container in a festive or appropriate style of paper, you now have an excellent holder to offer your wares in.

After you've canvassed all the obvious spaces (bedroom, kitchen, garage), take a look at the ones you missed. How about your yard or patio? Ready to relocate some lawn furniture, a forlorn pool, the bike no one rides, or the kiddie car no one races anymore? How about that over-crowded bed of iris, hostas, or daffodils that you could thin and then trade the excess bulbs? Itching to uproot a few shrubs and trade them for a rose bush or two in their place? Do you pay someone to mow your lawn but still own a lawn mower that's just gathering dust? This is an excellent item to barter, perhaps with the guy who cuts your grass or with the neighbors who could trade you leftover bulbs or veggies from their garden.

What about your pets? Now, before you think we're telling you to put Fluffy up for barter, consider this: When Karen was about ten years old, she had a tank of fish. When the fish would get too big for the tank, she would take them to the pet store she bought them from and trade them for different fish, often smaller. Larger fish are harder for pet stores to source, so Karen's trade not only provided a nice new fish inventory for the owners but also kept her own fish tank more diverse and interesting. And when one group of fish grew too large again, back to the pet store she'd go for another trade.

Years later, Karen's son Joe had a cat that never bonded with him; Joe was so disappointed that the cat wanted nothing to do with him. One day, Karen's husband, Rick, was chatting with a buddy about the situation, and the friend offered a solution. He had a Llewellin setter he had bred for hunting, but that dog just wouldn't hunt. He offered to trade the setter for the aloof feline. The new puppy and Joe were a better match, and the cat got a home where her snob-bish temperament was appreciated—a pet problem solved through barter.

Vehicles can play into your barter plans in interesting ways, depending on what you want to do with them. If you've got an old car that you aren't using, you could trade it for something you do want. If you have a vehicle that no longer suits your needs and is in good shape, you've got even more creative possibilities. Maybe your aging parents need a vehicle that has hand controls or other adaptive technology. Perhaps your family has grown, and you need to get rid of your sports car or motorcycle in favor of a van or family-friendly vehicle. By the same token, if your children have grown up and moved out, it's a great time to trade your SUV for a smaller car (and think of the gasoline you'll save).

Sometimes you'll want to trade a vehicle out of desire rather than necessity. Karen's husband, Rick, is a great example of that. Rick once bought a race car that was over-equipped for the type of racing he really wanted to do. If he had tried to trade it back in to the dealer, he would have gotten far less than he had paid for it. Instead, Rick offered to trade the car to a buddy who had a muscle car that was more to the specs Rick had in mind. They made the trade, and both were delighted with the exchange.

Some people have equipment like a backhoe, electric generator, trailer, bush hog, snowmobile, personal watercraft, or karaoke machine. Often that equipment isn't being operated 100 percent of the time, but you can make it work for you even when you aren't using it. It presents a couple of fantastic barter opportunities: You can either offer to perform work using the equipment or allow a trading partner to use the machinery without you. Either way, you put tools, implements, recreational vehicles, and other such equipment to work for you even when you aren't using it. Imagine the possibilities: You can trade your personal watercraft for time in someone's vacation home on the water. You can barter your karaoke machine for free drinks or meals at your favorite bar

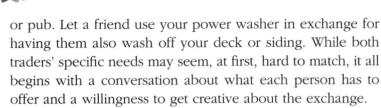

or pub. Let a friend use your power washer in exchange for having them also wash off your deck or siding. While both traders' specific needs may seem, at first, hard to match, it all begins with a conversation about what each person has to offer and a willingness to get creative about the exchange.

Most likely the big-ticket items for barter are easier to spot around your house, but did you also consider taking a closer look at your books, DVDs, games, and CDs? Those are all highly barterable items, and there are several great Web sites solely focused on entertainment that will give you venues for exchange. Just by listing a single item on a site like Swaptree.com, you could get access to hundreds of other items that people are willing to exchange, all for the cost of postage. This is especially helpful if you've got bookcases full of novels you won't read again, movies your kids have tired of or outgrown, and games that you've mastered. While we love our public libraries and various rental services, barter sites like these mean there's no need to worry about return dates or late fees. They take some of the stress out of everyday living. And when you're tired of them, you can trade them again for something new; now that's serious recycling.

There are also Web sites for trading unused gift cards. If you can't fathom ever redeeming that card from Aunt Ethel for the Fruitcake-of-the-Month Club, sites like CardAvenue.com or PlasticJungle.com allow you to trade for cards at the places you really do want to shop. You get the stuff you really want, and you don't have to figure out where to put all those fruitcakes. As an added layer of protection, these sites verify the amounts on the cards before the trade can happen, which is a bit more reassuring than just putting an offer on CraigsList.org.

If you want to add a social element to your barter experience, organize a neighborhood barter party. Neighborhoods like Sunnyside in Portland, Oregon, and Norwood, in Cincinnati, Ohio, have been doing just that. The structure of the neighborhood swap can vary greatly, depending on how the community wants it to transpire. In Sunnyside, for instance, everyone brings their stuff to a school gym where it's sorted by type. Volunteers who help with orchestrating the Useful Goods Exchange get first pick of the booty. Then the doors are thrown open, and the neighbors mosey through to pick up whatever they want. The swap works on the honor system, and the community loves it. In Norwood, the neighbors simply share whatever they have that others might need, such as a lawn mower or working in the community garden.

Another take would be for the neighbors to pick a date for a barter block party and then position all their stuff in their yards like a yard sale and then let the swapping begin. Each neighbor could use scrip for items "purchased" or "sold" if they don't feel that the honor system would work. Anything that isn't sold can be donated to charity.

Other neighborhood swaps focus on particular types of items: Halloween costumes, clothing, plants, bulbs, seeds, toys, sports equipment, books, movies, CDs, home accessories—you name it. In the end, everyone gets to trade away what they no longer want and replace it with something far more useful or desirable.

We would also recommend that you don't let barter stop at your home or neighborhood. Check out your workplace for trade fodder. Does your employer routinely throw out items like office furniture, electronics, raw materials, flawed/repairable merchandise, or other goods? If so, ask if you can take those items instead of tossing them into the waste stream. You'll not only be getting more great items for barter that will save you cash but also be helping the environment by recycling. You can help persuade your company to let you have its (ahem) trash by explaining that it will get to promote your recycling efforts within its industry and among employees as an earth-friendly practice. If the items you get come in a steady flow, you're in a stronger position to join a barter exchange and make trading easier.

If you really get enthusiastic about barter (and how could you not?), consider getting a job as a trade broker at an exchange. The industry is always looking for creative, energetic people who understand the positive impact that barter can have on people's lives. And how better to become an expert on barter than by being on the inside? You'll also have access to some of the juiciest trades around as they come up. (Check out chapter 11 for more about working in the barter industry.)

In the unlikely event that you are a neat freak and don't have much clutter lying about for bartering, you may want to start haunting garage and tag sales to find items that will cost you little and gain you much. While it might seem a bit illogical for barter mavens to recommend paying hard-won cash for castoffs at a yard sale, it's not a bad strategy. If you can improve what you buy to make it more valuable, or you've discovered a barter market for a particular sort of item (refurbished machinery/electronics or found-object art, perhaps), then you can actually earn more through trading than what you paid for the raw materials. A friend of Shera's is a very talented decorative painter who buys used or unlovely wooden objects at yard sales. Her husband strips or sands them, and she then paints them with her own delightfully creative designs. She trades and sells them at craft shows, which is an even more powerful use of what she finds. She generates cash and barter all while exercising her creative talents and doing what she loves.

You can apply the same idea to the many different objects that people toss aside, especially after home renovations or during mass moving periods such as month ends or the finish of college semesters. Items dumped in alleys, beside Dumpsters, or curbside can provide a wealth of barter possibilities free for the taking. Check your area's college calendars to discover when students are likely to be finishing the semester and moving.

You can also look for area-wide large-item disposal days when the pickings will be excellent. Make sure that if you're trolling for large objects you've got extra hands and an appropriate truck or other vehicle to haul the goods away. If the renovation castoffs are being dumped in a construction trash container, a good policy is to ask before you do any Dumpster diving. While you're on pretty safe ground assuming that the objects are no longer wanted, you don't want to run afoul of hazardous materials in the bin or startled home owners shocked to see you making off with their old chandeliers. Besides, you may find that by asking, there's even better stuff yet to go into the bin that they'll let you take before it hits the Dumpster and takes more of a beating.

To find additional hidden barter opportunities in your life, don't forget about the spaces outside your residence. Do you have a storage unit crammed full of furniture, kitchenware, and unused appliances? How much of it do you really need? Are there boxes or shelves of items at your mom's house that you've forgotten about? Many people own boats, campers, RVs, or aircraft that they can't afford or no longer want to operate. Instead of racking up storage or rental fees, look for chances to barter those items. Or you can barter time using them if the market is flooded or you really don't want to give them up. Just be sure to check with your insurer about any special riders, as you may need to cover other users if you opt to barter time using the item rather than trading it away.

When it comes to the stuff that fills your life, just be creative and don't rule out any possibilities. You never know what may arise.

TRADE YOUR TALENT

Take a look at your hands. Whoa! There's some serious barter power there, as well as with your legs, your throat, your arms. But most of all, your greatest barter potential is your mind. What you've got lying around your house or garage is one group of potential trades, but you also have vast realms of barter possibilities that you probably haven't considered within your own time and talents. Before you start nay-saying—"But I don't have any talents!"—listen to this: You don't have to be a concert pianist or a Hollywood actor to have talent. Your talents are often the activities you adore that you don't get paid for . . . the things you love to do simply because you enjoy them. Do you love to collect stamps or coins? There are lots of barter opportunities in your collection. Do you crochet, quilt, or do some other handicraft? Fantastic trades are at your fingertips, quite literally. The work of your hands is barterable.

Deborah Hyland is a perfect example. Deborah loves to knit—but she doesn't do just any sort of knitting. Deborah is a Civil War reenactor and has developed a niche for herself, knitting Civil War–era reproduction goods. She trades her handiwork with other reenactor craftsmen for an astounding assortment of period pieces. She's traded for custom-made taffeta boots that would have cost her $200 if she had paid cash. She has also traded her extraordinary nightcaps, shawls, socks, and other knit clothing. Her creations take hours (one sock requires ten hours of knitting), and she uses heavier-grade yarn and more-complex period designs than modern knits typically call for. Her tip for working out the value of a trade with another craftsman is to explain about the quality of the raw materials and how many hours are required to make the piece. Then she lets the buyer determine what he or she will offer to trade in return. That way, everyone feels that the exchange is fair, and it tends to be based more on hours of workmanship rather than dollar value. In the end, both traders get handmade reproductions that would have cost hundreds, maybe thousands, of dollars in the cash market.

Do you love to hunt, fish, or garden? You can trade an extra fish, duck, deer, watermelon, or quail for the things you don't have. The game or produce that your family can't consume can become barter material. You could even be strategic about it and plant more, fish more, or bag an extra animal so that you are certain to have food to barter. As the demand for organic food skyrockets, you could bring home some lucrative trades for what you fish, hunt, or grow.

When we said your talent might be in your legs or throat, we weren't exaggerating. What we meant is that you can barter your physical skills, talents, and abilities in a wide spectrum of services. For example, instead of being just an exercise fanatic, you could become someone's personal trainer. Or think about using your vocal talents to sing at events or give motivational speeches. Whatever you are passionate about is a contender when it comes to bartering your talents.

Often you'll find that your workplace skills are also barter worthy. Because she has been a business owner, Karen is able to draw on her knowledge and her gift for coaching to help entrepreneurs have more profitable companies and more personal satisfaction with their work. She has traded coaching for restaurant certificates, Christmas decorating, feng shui, housecleaning, chiropractic care, hypnotherapy, and more. In some cases, she trades for chores she dislikes, such as cleaning her home. Besides allowing Karen to not have to do her own cleaning, the trade frees her up to do more of the work she loves, including work that brings in cash. Karen could easily spend all day coaching clients and doing what she is passionate about because it doesn't feel like work.

Beyond your talents, you can also barter your time and labor. If you need someone to paint your house, trade your time babysitting the painter's children for his labor. Your labor doesn't have to be highly skilled. Trade housecleaning for handyman services, yard work for cooking, auto detailing for gutter cleaning, or whatever physical labor your can perform. Just recognize that the lower the level of skill you trade, the more hours you will probably have to put into it if you are bartering for a higher-level skill, such as accounting or legal work.

There's one other skill that you should consider bartering: your knowledge. What you know can be converted into a heavy-duty amount of barter depending on your area of expertise. For example, are you fluent in a language other than English? You can barter language lessons. Are you a talented cake decorator? Teach newbies how to bake scrumptious cakes and decorate them like a celebrity pastry chef. Do you understand the movements of the planets and stars? Teach others how to become budding astronomers—or, if your knowledge is focused on the astral plane, trade astrological readings for clients. Dare we say that the sky's the limit on how you apply the fruits of your knowledge to bartering?

TIME TO MAKE A LIST

To get started figuring out what your talents are, make a list of your hobbies, pastimes, activities that you enjoy, and work skills. What do you love to do? Ask other people what they think your talents and skills are. Is there something that you enjoyed doing when you were a child, teenager, or young adult that you haven't thought of in years? Could you do it now as barter? Perhaps you've got a skill that you could develop a bit more to turn it into a trade, such as turning sewing into tailoring or upholstering. Do you love to shop? Become someone's personal shopper. Do you love to cook? Relieve a bit of the pressure around the holidays and trade your cooking skills with a neighbor for some much-needed housecleaning. There is a nearly unlimited list of possibilities to consider.

Once you have your inventory, ask yourself which thing you'd like to do the most and/or what would bring you the most in trade. If you're not sure what skill is most in demand, check out some of the barter Web sites to see what people need. It's a safe bet that those are the highly sought-after services. Also check to see what is available in abundance. If a dozen people in your area are offering housecleaning, you might be better served by offering something different or offering an unusual version of it. Instead of general house-cleaning, offer deep- or spring-cleaning services. That sort of differentiation can measurably increase how many trades come your way.

But we don't want you to have all the fun alone. Ask your spouse/partner and kids if they want to join in. Make a skills and labor inventory with them. You might be surprised what they are willing to do once they realize what bartering can bring them. Your children might make great babysitters, dog walkers, lawn mowers, elder sitters, tutors, fish-tank cleaners, car detailers, or gardeners, depending on their age and likes. It's possible that the whole family could barter one activity together. Does everyone in your crew love birthday parties? What about offering a party-on-demand service? Mom bakes the cake and goodies, Dad procures supplies and dresses up like a clown, the kids plan and direct party games, and everyone cleans up.

While it might be tempting to force your kids to barter their labor, unless your family's situation isn't dire, we don't recommend it. When people choose to offer a labor out of what they love, you'll get less resistance and more barter hours from them simply because they enjoy it. Attraction is a better policy than compulsion. Reward is a strong incentive as well. If kids see what barter can produce for them, they'll be more eager to become barter babies. It also helps take the pressure off Mom and Dad. Think of all the times your children have whined for this or that. With barter, saying "no" turns into "What can you barter for that?"

Plus, barter is a great life skill to teach your children. They'll learn what the value of their labor is worth, discover that it can be equated to more than the dollar, and forge a sense of self-reliance rather than victimhood that will serve them well for the rest of their years and for generations to come.

After you've made a skills inventory and rounded up the goods you have available to barter, make a wish list of your needs and wants. Take a look at your personal budget and prioritize the list by needs first. You may not be able to barter for necessities, but it helps to put your energy into getting your needs met before the desires of your heart. If the desires are what you get offers for first, you'll still save cash. But keep in mind that when you are trading labor, you have a finite amount of barterable time. If you sell your time for wants rather than needs, your fixed expenses won't shrink, you may miss out on some stress relief, and you'll find that you don't have enough capacity to take advantage of an offer that could fill a high-priority need.

THE THREESOME

Some people will find that they don't have much stuff, or they have a limited amount of time, or they have a trading partner with a specific need they can't meet. Time to take a hard look at who's sitting on your bench. Someone else in your life may be able to fulfill a specific need a prospective trading partner has but that you lack. These sorts of third-party, or triangulation, trades can come to your rescue. Yes, third-party trades do complicate a transaction, but they can come together well if all the parties communicate clearly and specifically and, most important, everyone executes his or her side of the deal.

Shera's first foray into barter was a third-party deal. After she got engaged she realized that to have the wedding she really wanted, she would need to get creative. At the time, she was a newspaper reporter, and trading her writing skills for goods would have been unethical. She couldn't think of another skill or talent that would be worthy of acquiring her dream wedding, but she did have a great connection that could get the job done. Her stepfather owned a tiny little newspaper outside her hometown of Nashville, Tennessee, and he bartered advertising space for goods and services all the time. A quick phone call and she had her stepdad's agreement that he would provide as much ad space to trade as she needed. She got a copy of his ad rate sheet so she knew how much cash value she could work with. Then she got busy with the Yellow Pages (pre-Internet times, folks) and started looking for wedding shops, florists, and printers in her parents' little town.

She found a wedding shop nearby, an independent store that would have more flexibility than a large retail chain. She knew she needed to call the owner and see if she could work out a deal, but she'd never sold anything in her life (not counting lightbulbs and Christmas wrapping paper for the high school band). How was she supposed to call up a rank stranger, make this outrageous proposal to someone who didn't know her from Adam or Eve, and snag the most beautiful wedding gown of her dreams?

Nervous as a long-tailed cat in a room full of rocking chairs, she mustered up her courage and made the call. She stuttered like someone with a mouthful of marbles and was anything but smooth. But the store owner agreed to meet to talk over her proposal. Several weeks later, they hashed out a deal with a handshake, and she got to pick out a beautiful white dress, veil, and blue garter.

Heady with this success, she worked the same maneuver with a florist (again, with nerves rattling). She bartered her way into a stunning armful of roses, bouquets for her brides-maids, and boutonnieres for the groom and groomsmen. In all, she saved about $1,500 by bartering and eliminated a huge financial strain.

That's just one iteration of a third-party trade. Traditionally, the term "three-way trade" has described a complex transaction where one party traded with a partner who provided goods to a third trader that actually produced the goods the original party desired. It looks like this: Jim needs someone to power wash his deck, and he can offer his auto mechanic skills in exchange. Don can do the power washing but doesn't need any car repairs. Don's fellow church member Lucy has an older car that needs work, but she has no money for the repairs. Since Lucy is a great housekeeper, she offers to clean Don's house in exchange for the repairs that he'll earn by trading power washing with Jim. Whew! Got all that? Basically it boils down to each party trading for what another party needs in relatively equal measure. Often, these types of trades work best when two of the parties know each other and can help hold each other accountable. But just as in a third-party barter, three-way trades can arise when a trader has a need but can't satisfy a trading partner with that good or service. Most of all, three-way trades take patience and creativity. But with persistence, traders can make them a win-win-win situation.

BALANCING THE PROS AND CONS

On balance, barter is more of a benefit than not for people with a bit of patience, flexibility, and determination. If you are aware of the downsides before you start, barter becomes a great gift. But it truly helps to be strategic about it. When you are, you'll suddenly discover that there is more flexibility and fun in a life that's far more enjoyable to live.

GREAT TRADE!

Stacey Kannenberg's dear friend Alison was strapped for cash and needed an attorney to help her get a divorce. As it happened, the lawyer that Alison wanted to hire had written a manuscript that she wanted to turn into a book. Alison had public relations experience but that alone wasn't enough to cover the attorney fees or what the lawyer really needed—someone to help her self-publish and market her book. So Stacey offered to throw in her savvy as a book marketing and branding expert, and Alison provided the public relations expertise. Voilà! A third-party barter was born. But then the deal got even better. Because of the amount of help Alison's attorney needed to promote her book so that she could widely establish herself as an expert in her particular area of the law, Alison and Stacey both earned cash for the work they provided beyond the value of the legal work. Stacey helped her friend not only get a divorce for no cash but also attract a paying client. Stacey estimates that the total value of the deal in cash and barter was worth around $100,000. And, as icing on the cake, the two dear friends got to work together.

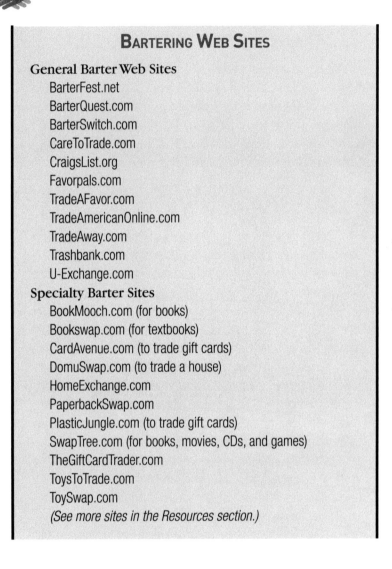

BARTERING WEB SITES

General Barter Web Sites
BarterFest.net
BarterQuest.com
BarterSwitch.com
CareToTrade.com
CraigsList.org
Favorpals.com
TradeAFavor.com
TradeAmericanOnline.com
TradeAway.com
Trashbank.com
U-Exchange.com

Specialty Barter Sites
BookMooch.com (for books)
Bookswap.com (for textbooks)
CardAvenue.com (to trade gift cards)
DomuSwap.com (to trade a house)
HomeExchange.com
PaperbackSwap.com
PlasticJungle.com (to trade gift cards)
SwapTree.com (for books, movies, CDs, and games)
TheGiftCardTrader.com
ToysToTrade.com
ToySwap.com
(See more sites in the Resources section.)

BARTER OPPORTUNITIES IN YOUR LIFE

Here is a list of the potential items and services you may have that could be bartered. This is not a comprehensive list; no list ever could be. But it will give you some ideas that you may not have considered and some clues you may have missed.

Stuff

Adult clothing
Antiques
Art (painting, sculpture, ceramics, photographs, etc.—yours or someone else's)
Baby clothes
Baby equipment
Baby furniture
Backhoes
Baking supplies or unused kitchen equipment
Beauty supplies
Bedding
Beds
Bicycles
Billiard or pool table
Boats
Bonds
Books
Bowling ball
Boxes for moving
Bridesmaid dress
Bulldozers
Bush hog
Camping supplies
Canoe or raft
Cars
CDs

Children's clothing
Clothing accessories
Coins or any other type of collectible
Comic books
Commodities
Computer peripherals
Computer/video games
Condo rentals
Cruises
Decor items
Discarded or extra building supplies
Dog supplies
Doghouses
Dogs
Dolls
DVDs
Engines
Event tickets
Fabric remnants
Fill dirt
Film cameras
Fish
Fixtures
Flowers (plants or bulbs)
Furniture
Furs
Game consoles
Garage space
Garden equipment

Garden supplies
Gift cards or certificates
Golf clubs and equipment
Guns
Handmade candles
Handmade jewelry
Hay, milk, seeds, or other
    agricultural products
Herbs
Homemade baked goods
Homemade dog treats
Honey
Horseback riding equipment
Horses
Ice skates
Leather
Livestock
Meals
Medicinal herbs
Musical instruments
Office supplies
Old wedding or engagement
    rings
Other unused jewelry
Outgrown children's
    clothing
Paint
Parking space
Pets
Planes
Pool supplies
Produce
Quilts
Race cars
Radios

Record albums
Recreational vehicles
Rocks
Roller skates
Rollerblades
Room and board
Rototiller
Scuba equipment
Sculptures
Seeds
Sewing machine
Sheds
Skateboards
Skis
Software
Sound equipment
Sports equipment, outgrown
    or unused (tennis rackets,
    golf clubs, in-line skates,
    etc.)
Stamps
Stocks
Storage space
Surfboards
Textbooks
Toiletries
Tools
Toys
Trailers
Unused computers and
    equipment
Used tennis balls, golf balls,
    or baseballs
Vacation homes
Vehicle parts

Wading pool
Wedding gown
Wine
Workout videos/DVDs
Yarn or other handiwork
    supplies

Talents/Skills/Services

Accounting
Acupuncture
Adventure guide
Advertising
Aftermarket vehicle installa-
    tion
Alternative healing
Appraisals (antiques, real
    estate, comic books,
    other areas of expertise)
Aquarium maintenance
Architecture
Artistic work
Astrology readings
Auditing
Auto repair
Babysitting
Babysitting co-op
Baking
Bartending
Beekeeping
Birthday party organizer
Boating/sailing (lessons or
    captaining)
Bookkeeping
Bulldozing

Cabinetmaking
Card dealer
Caretaking of animals or
    pets
Carving
Cat sitting
Catering
Chauffeur
Chef or cooking skills
Child care
Cleaning
Clothing design
Coaching (business and
    sports)
Cobbler
Computer purchasing
    consulting
Computer repair/service
Computer repair, upgrades,
    installations
Computer troubleshooting
Construction/building
Construction supervision
Cooking
Cooking instruction
Counseling
Crocheting
Dance performance or
    instruction
Data processing
Deaf interpreting
Deliveries
Dentistry
Dog walking

Drywall installation and
   repair
Editing/proofreading
Elder care
Elder companion
Electrical
Electronics repair
Emcee
Energy audits
Engineering
Errands
Event planning
Farming
Fashion consultant
Financial planning
Fishing excursions
Fishing lessons
Floral arrangement
Foreign language instruction
Foreign language inter-
   preting
Funeral officiant
Furniture refinishing
Furniture repair
Gardening
General repairs
Golf instruction
Graphic design
Green home consulting
Gymnastic instruction
Hair braiding
Haircutting/ hair styling
Handicrafts
Handyman

Health care
House-sitting
Hunting
Hypnotherapy
Interior design
Introductions to influential
   or business people
Inventing/prototyping
Janitorial service
Jewelry creation or repair
Junk hauling
Kayaking lessons
Knitting
Landscape design, construc-
   tion, or architecture
Laundry service
Lawn care
Legal
Livestock
Local tour guide
Locksmith
Makeup consultant
Marketing or other business
   consulting
Martial arts instruction
Massage
Matchmaking
Medical care
Model building
Modeling
Motorcycle repair
Mountaineering/climbing/
   adventure leader
Muralist

Musician
Nurse's aide
Nursing
Nutrition consulting
Optician
Organizing
Orthodontics
Painting (artistic, home, business)
Palm reading
Parachuting instruction
Pest control
Pharmaceutical consulting
Photography
Piano repair
Piano tuning
Plant care
Plumbing
Podiatry
Pond installation
Pool service
Power washing
Psychic readings
Raising animals
Real estate broker/agent
Recording, using your home audio suite
Referee
Reflexology
Reptiles
Research
Retirement planning

RV repair, storage, restoration
Sailboat rental
Sailboat cruises
Sailing lessons
Sales
Scrapbooking
Sculpting lessons
Search engine optimization
Secretarial services
Self-defense instruction
Setting up sales for people on Web sites such as eBay
Skating instruction
Ski instruction (snow or water)
Social networking communications
Solar installation
Sound system installation
Speech therapy
Stump grinding
Surfing instruction
Surgery
Surveying
Swimming instruction
Tailoring
Tarot readings
Tatooing
Tax filing
Taxidermy
Teaching

Travel service
Tree trimming
Trivia night host/question
    creator
Trucking
Tutoring
Upholstery
Upholstery instruction
Vehicle purchase consulting
Veterinary care
Video editing
Video production
Videography

Weaving
Web site development
Wedding officiant
Wedding planning
Welding
Window installation
Wine consultant/party host
Wood chopping
Woodworking
Woodworking instruction
Writing
Writing instruction

 **CHAPTER 3**

TRADING LIKE A PRO

Become a possibilitarian. No matter how dark things seem to be or actually are, raise your sights and see possibilities—always see them, for they're always there.

—Dr. Norman Vincent Peale

Now that we've whetted your appetite for barter, you're probably raring to go. First, a quick definition: Barter is the exchange of goods or services without cash. (Yes, it's true that sometimes cash becomes part of the transaction, but we'll get into that later on.) Barter is not haggling, although some people think it's the same thing. Haggling is negotiating the price of a good or service. So while haggling can be part of barter, they are not one and the same. And whether haggling is involved or not, barter at its roots is simple, which is part of its wonderful appeal.

Another couple of definitions that are helpful to know are direct barter and exchange-based or commercial barter. *Direct barter* is trade between two people or organizations without a broker or middleman involved. *Exchange-based* or *commercial barter* is barter between two people or organizations with a company or broker who facilitates the deal.

To get started, you'll need to take that assessment of what you've got to offer from chapter 2 and take a look at what you can do (singing, marketing, repair), what you have (goods), and what you know (teaching Spanish, lecturing about gardening). What you do, have, and know are the basis of what you will be able to offer in trade.

Once you've compiled a list of items, knowledge, or labor that you can offer, give some thought to how much those goods or services are worth. Assign a cash value to it; even if it's an object that seems nearly worn-out, it probably has some cash value to someone. If you're an excellent carpenter, the value of an hour of your carpentry skills will be what is generally paid on the free market in your area for your skill level. If you're more of a shade-tree carpenter, you should value your skills at less than the prevailing union rates. When you assign a value to something, you must take into consideration its condition; what the fair market value is; what people have been paying for similar items in stores, on the Internet, and at eBay; and how much demand there is for it. Those factors will affect the ultimate value you place on a good or service.

Although we've asked you to assign a dollar value to what you do, know, and have, take a moment to consider that your earning potential isn't tied to your paycheck (assuming you're getting one right now). It's tied to what you can generate in all forms—including what you can barter. How wonderful to realize that your worth is not that net earnings figure on your pay stub. You have immensely more earning potential than you realize, and that understanding becomes much clearer when you begin bartering. In a small way, barter can help elevate your self-worth a bit.

Now it's time to hunt for trading partners. It's best to approach barter as a flow of opportunities rather than a pure shopping trip. This is less like going to the shopping mall and more like popping open your friend's closet to see if she's got anything she wants to swap. Barter is all about establishing and building relationships, even those you'll form with strangers, and keeping them content as you barter, perhaps again and again with the same individual.

Barter opportunities are most readily available through Internet sites, but you aren't limited to the Web. The good news is that the world is wonderfully broader than it used to be, and barter goes faster than when Karen owned her own barter exchange in the 1980s and 1990s. Back then, the Internet wasn't a factor like it is today. An individual had a much more difficult time finding trading partners, and barter was a much slower process. Traders had to rely on bulletin boards, newspaper ads, chance encounters, barter clubs, and direct offers to swap. Those are all still viable options in the Internet age, but now there are many excellent trading partners who are far easier to connect with on Web sites such as CraigsList.org, BarterQuest.com, and U-Exchange.com. Check out these sites, along with local bulletin boards (real or virtual), newspapers, your e-mail list, Meetup.com, church groups, social clubs, or anywhere else you find people. Be bold. Put your offer out there.

A WEB OF BARTER

For Internet trading, your first area of concern is the headline or title you give your listing. Be specific about what you're offering, and maybe add a descriptive word or two to boost interest. An example would be *"never-worn* wedding gown" or "Tiffany-style lamp, NWT" (new with tags). Add the location of the good or service, unless it's a service that is readily available to clients nationwide, such as graphic design. Location is critical for items that can't be shipped or are too expensive to move by postal mail or UPS. It's also important for services that are area specific or limited, such as babysitting, lawn care, or vacation home rental.

When using barter Web sites, you should be specific and descriptive about what you're offering to trade. Instead of listing a "2005 Ford Focus," try "2005 Ford Focus in Mint Condition, Low Miles, Bose Stereo, New Tires." Which car listing are you more likely to click on? Just because you are trading doesn't mean you shouldn't use eye-catching strategies from eBay.com or classified ads. Selling is selling, even if you are bartering. Your headline is critical to attracting attention immediately and standing out from the crowd of traders who are also offering cars. In the body of your barter listing, make sure you give as much detail as possible. Give the viewer plenty of reasons to contact you and begin the barter dialogue.

Photos are helpful, if not essential. Make sure they show the item from key angles and are of good quality. A good model is eBay, which has perfected the art of the online resale. Just as you would at eBay, note if there are flaws in the item. You should show them so that the viewer can see exactly what he or she is purchasing. This way, you will not only have an informed partner on your hands but also be establishing trust by showing everything, warts and all. You also eliminate the risk of a buyer later claiming that the flaws were hidden. For a service such as home repair or hairstyling, you may be able to take before-and-after photos to demonstrate your capabilities. Post a photo of yourself on sites that allow pictures. This sort of personalization fits perfectly with the atmosphere of barter. Since this is a person-to-person interaction, personality matters—even over the Web. We all prefer to deal with someone who is more than just a name and an account on the Internet; your photo is just one more way to engender trust.

Depending on the nature of the trading site, you should list your own Web site or blog, if you have one. An Internet presence shows that you are more professional and not a fly-by-night trader. Again, this is just more fodder to add to the bank of trust you are building. By listing a link to your Web site, you are able to supply even more detail about your goods or services, providing testimonials and direct contact information on your site. If you are a service provider, put your résumé on the trading site, or, if that's not possible, let viewers know it's available for downloading through e-mail or on your blog or Web site.

Consider whether urgency will be an element of the trade. While most trades are going to be for goods and services that have no particular shelf life, there are some that stick around for only a brief while. If what you are offering has a time limit on its availability, make sure you indicate that in either the title/headline of your listing or early on in your description. Limited-time offers such as a vacation home rental could slip by without a taker if you don't promote the necessity of acting quickly on your offer. The same thing applies for produce, puppies, tickets to events, or anything that can age beyond desirability or usefulness.

If there are limits to your offer, you'll save yourself a lot of misunderstanding and grief if you are clear about what they are. If you are offering a service, make sure you spell out exactly what you will and won't do. (Example: "Home-based child care, ages six weeks and up. No nights or weekends.") If there are aspects of what you do that require paying cash for a related service, mention that as well so that there is as little confusion as possible.

While we mentioned earlier that you should affix a value to what you are offering, keep in mind that it might vary by region. You may need to visit CraigsList.org or look at regional publications like your town's newspaper to get a sense of regional values. Not sure exactly what the market value is? Then you'll need to surf over to sites like eBay.com and Amazon.com to expand your research. Stores and catalogs are certainly other venues to check. Just remember that the value of the trade is based on *current* market value, not what you paid for it. That should take into consideration the condition of the item, if the market is flooded with it or not, what others are paying for it, limited-time availability, and other similar factors.

When it comes to what you want to barter for, again, being specific is more likely to land you a trade than being general. Saying "open to whatever" may seem like the right signal to send to show that you're willing to discuss anything reasonable. But are you *truly* open to anything? Can you really use a gross of brussels sprouts? Failing to list two or three specific items you desire (and preferably far more) means that someone who has the thing you want will not be able to find you in a keyword search—and then you've missed out on a trade. The key is to provide detailed information (without going overboard) while at the same time expressing openness to offers for goods/services that you haven't listed as wants. In many ways, Internet barter is about casting a wide net that expresses flexibility along with specifics. The more flexible you are, the more "big fish" you'll land. Just stand out in the pond a bit by listing what kinds of "fish" you most want.

TIMING AND THE APPROACH

Consider trading for an item or service during the off-season for that particular good or service. People often don't think to purchase boats, landscaping, time at a beach house, pool maintenance, or a new deck during the winter, but that's exactly when you should be offering to trade on such seasonal items. Businesses or the owner/provider of those items are often less busy at those times, and you'll get a warmer reception to the barter discussion than you would during the high season when there's more demand, or they have customers with cash in hand clamoring at their doors. That doesn't mean you have to plan your vacation at the beach in December if you're going to be shivering your beach balls off. But you are more likely to have a fruitful negotiation if you broach the discussion in the off-season. You can negotiate for the optimal time to stay, perhaps several months down the road.

Since barter isn't like buying something off the shelf, your approach to a prospective trader can make all the difference in whether the trade happens or not. If you're in do-or-die mode, a prospective partner might be frightened off by your tenseness. No one enjoys dealing with desperate people, and that level of angst kills your ability to creatively think about how to make the deal work. While barter is, simply, the exchange of one thing for another, it's also a social interaction, which is crucial to keep in mind. We've seen people come into an exchange with a sense of entitlement or a superior attitude that was off-putting to their potential partner. The end result was a dead deal and bad feelings on one or both person's parts.

And when it comes to actual negotiating, don't denigrate what the other person is offering in an attempt to cut a better deal. This is more about making a match than beating the best bargain out of an adversary. Common sense and basic courtesy should be your guiding lights. For example, if you make an appointment to look over the items to be traded, keep the appointment and be on time. While it seems obvious that you should treat others the way you'd like to be treated, we've seen plenty of people act otherwise. Friendly, interested, open-minded, and respectful are the best attitudes to adopt in any trade, and you'll find that this will lead to greater rewards.

CHECKING IT OUT

When an offer is on the table, don't just grab it blindly. Treat any deal like you would a cash transaction in terms of the research you do and the questions you ask. Depending on what you're trading for, you should ask

- how old it is,
- what condition it's in,
- whether the trader owns it or if there are outstanding loans in force,
- whether there are any cash outlays involved,
- whether the item has ever been damaged, or
- if there's any other pertinent information you should know.

If you're seeking a service, check out the provider first. Call professional licensing agencies, or check listings online if they're available, to ensure that the individual is in good standing with regulators, such as state dental or physicians' boards. Look online or call the Better Business Bureau to see if any complaints have been filed and, if so, how they were resolved. Ask for references from the trader and call them. It also helps to ask these customers detailed questions about what sort of work was done for them and if there were any hiccups along the way. Just asking if they were satisfied with the provider won't necessarily solicit the details you need to make an informed choice.

Be careful to avoid over- or undervaluing the trade. You might be tempted to nudge up the value just to get more in return, or perhaps you have some sort of emotional connection to the item and you're having a hard time letting it go. Overvaluation truly goes against the trusting spirit of barter. While you might be lucky at trading for more than you offered a few times, your trading partners will eventually realize that you're overcharging and go elsewhere to barter.

If your trading partner is the one who seems to be asking for too much in exchange, your knowledge of the fair market value of the items or services involved will help you bargain more effectively. When Karen was trading with a restaurant to hold her son's wedding rehearsal dinner, knowing the value of the deal came in handy. The husband and wife owners of the restaurant said they were willing to trade but that they would accept half cash/half barter for the dinner. Karen, who used trade credits that she had earned from business consulting and workshops through a barter company, could clearly see the value of the trade because all of the prices were printed on the menu. There was no need to haggle over the cost. The deal worked out well for everyone involved, and Karen's son and new daughter-in-law were thrilled with their rehearsal dinner feast. Karen and Rick were thrilled to be able to provide a memorable event for the family while also easing the strain on their wallets.

If the deal is unequal (and many times deals are, at least to a degree) and you need to offer more to make it work, you've got a couple of options:

1) You can throw another item or service into the mix. If you're asking a handyman to build a deck in trade for

your cleaning his house every other week, and he can justify that the deal is slanted in your favor, offer to sit for his kids or elderly parent for an appropriate number of hours to make up the difference.

2) If you've offered everything you have available to trade, it might be time to pry out your wallet and sweeten the deal with some cash. Nothing prevents cash from being part of the mix as long as you're happy with the combined offer. Just be clear on all aspects of the deal before you shake on it. If you are paying out more in cash than the retail value of the item, that's probably a bad trade.

The great thing about direct barter is that it's not absolutely necessary to have complicated legal contracts, lawyers, or elaborate sales tickets to seal a deal. While those elements can definitely be part of a trade (nations such as Russia and China certainly wouldn't barter without them), a simple handshake, verbal agreement, or e-mail is all that's necessary for most transactions. The exception would be if you're trading for big-ticket items. A short, straightforward contract is a good idea in those instances. A contract can be as simple as sending an e-mail confirming what the trade is, the value of it, and the conditions for how it will happen (trading ten haircuts over a year for painting a living room, for instance). Summarizing the details helps to solidify the trade and avoid confusion later on if a dispute arises. (See a sample contract in the Resources section.) Barter is inherently about trust, and most of the experienced traders we know operate with that mind-set. However, they also use good common sense when making a trade. If an exchange is generally equitable and all parties feel that they are getting a fair shake, the deal is a good one.

So how do you protect yourself when exchanging goods if you aren't in the same area? If your item is small enough to send through the mail, a little insurance can't hurt, in case the postal service loses it. It also helps to send the item via certified mail to prove that it actually arrived as you promised. If the item has a high value, such as jewelry, you might be better served sending it via UPS, FedEx, or another carrier that tracks every single package.

Once you've concluded a deal, it's a good idea to record each trade. You can keep a log of whom you've traded with, including contact information, date and value of the trade, what you swapped, and how much cash was involved, if any. If you love your computer, keep up with your trades by using QuickBooks, a spreadsheet, or whatever tool works best for you. Tracking is essential if you are self-employed and your barter is related to that employment because there are tax consequences (more on that later) to your trade. Logging your trades is also helpful because you may have the same item to trade again and want to look back at your previous deals as a reference point. You also get to prove how much cash you've saved and congratulate yourself on all of those great trades you've concluded. What a confidence builder!

CO-OPS AND BARTER COMMUNITIES

Trading doesn't have to be about just stuff and services. You can trade your kids. Well, not really. But you *can* trade taking care of your children. Many parents are familiar with the babysitting co-op, although they may not have such a formal name for it. These types of co-ops are just another form of barter. They're popular in many areas because they give parents a ready source of trustworthy adult babysitters and no need to fork over a wad of cash to the sitter at the end of a night out. Babysitting co-ops work best with at least five families who live in fairly close proximity to each other. As a parent, you'll have to determine if you are comfortable sitting for the variety of ages and numbers of children in a single family. If you aren't comfortable caring for another couple's infant along with their twin toddlers, you may not be a good fit for that particular co-op. But don't despair. Look for another one, or, if you can't find one, start your own! Let barter empower you.

Expect some preliminaries before you are admitted to a co-op where you aren't well-known to everyone in the group. Before a family is admitted to the co-op, the other members want to be confident that they can trust their children to be safe with every parent. New members often join by invitation only so that absolute strangers aren't in the group. Some co-ops require a few home visits before they admit members, and others even go so far as to do a background check before admitting new members, which is easily done by becoming a block- or safe-home program member. Background checks are also available on a variety of Web sites that provide the information for a small fee.

When forming a co-op, members should develop rules of conduct. For instance, you'll need to decide if overnight sitting is permitted, how sick children will be handled, and who will keep track of the hours earned and spent. Some co-op members pay each other in scrip that they design or some other form of currency, such as raffle tickets or poker chips. (You can even personalize it with photos of kids or toys.) New members are often given a set amount of scrip to begin trading with. The scrip can be issued in varying denominations, such as fifteen-, thirty-, and sixty-minute increments. Sitters earn additional scrip if they care for more than one child at a time. Some co-ops allow members to charge more scrip if the care is provided in the children's home rather than the caregiver's house. Some clubs have regular meetings to discuss issues, resolve concerns, and check to see that parents aren't being overlooked for sitting opportunities. If a sitter isn't getting many requests, the co-op members make note of it and try to call on that sitter more often. The rules for each co-op are best set by its members according to their particular concerns and values, and the rules may evolve as the members' needs change.

Another form of grassroots organized bartering is the barter fair (or faire). These are grand community events that marry the joy of live musical performances, the energy of dancing, the delights of festival food, a variety of vendors' sales booths, and the art of bartering. Some even include camping, group healing sessions, massage, teaching, and demonstrations. One of the biggest draws to the barter fair beyond the entertainment value is the presence of local farmers who come to sell or barter their produce. Fairgoers can get great fresh fruits, vegetables, and proteins—sometimes organic—just by bartering.

Some barter fairs will have a "freecycle" table of donated goods that fairgoers can pick through to select a few items and then barter with them for vendors' products. Freecycle tables allow people to clean out their closets/garages/and so on, provide some grist for the barter mill, and generate goodwill among the crowd by providing freebies that can be put to good use through recycling. Often kids will grab a few items at the freecycle table, which gives them a chance to learn about bartering.

Another community-building aspect of barter fairs is that they are often organized and set up by volunteers who get free admission to the fair in exchange for a few hours of their labor. They may do anything from setting up a stage, installing a temporary kitchen, emptying garbage, selling tickets, or breaking down equipment and cleaning up after the fair is over.

Perhaps the biggest difference between a barter fair and a flea market or swap meet is that barter fairs tend to attract more homemade arts and crafts compared to mass-market-produced goods that so frequently populate flea markets. The barter fair culture is also more free-spirited, earthy, and equitable than the decidedly commercial flea market. You're more likely to see campers dancing around a bonfire at a barter fair versus suburban housewives shopping for kitchen gadgets or country kitsch. No matter the spirit behind the event, barter is still the basis, and it's an entertaining way to spend a weekend with the family and get to know other like-minded traders.

In essence, direct barter can take on a variety of forms and venues, but it all boils down to one thing: two or more people exchanging things they value. The added benefits are building a stronger community, saving money, recycling, solving problems, and getting to know your next new friend.

GREAT TRADE!

Hugh Simpson gets our honorary title of Barter King. Hugh, who lives in Tellico Plains, Tennessee, had a whopper of a trade from the very start of his barter career in the 1980s. Hugh loves plying his skills as a public relations expert, and he's pretty creative with it. So when Maggie, a kitchen designer in Atlanta, offered to trade with him for his PR help, he was certainly willing to listen. At that early stage of her career, Maggie couldn't afford Hugh's $100-an-hour price tag, but she had an intriguing offer. Her ex-husband had a side business importing Mercedes-Benz sedans from Germany to the United States. He had a customer who was getting ready to trade in his 1973 Mercedes for a new one. Maggie offered to trade the used Mercedes for twenty-five hours of Hugh's work.

"Done!" said Hugh, who was dragging around in a beat-up Pontiac and knew that a pricey Mercedes would certainly make his stock go up with the opposite sex.

In short order, a then-hot-to-trot Hugh was tooling around in a swanky Mercedes, and Maggie got top-notch public relations assistance that helped propel her to a career as one of the most sought-after kitchen designers in town. Maggie saved time by not having to clean up the car, advertise it, field calls, or meet prospective buyers. Hugh didn't have to pay sales tax on the car or search for just the right vehicle to suit his needs. Hugh's only regret is that he didn't hang on to that car over the years. He estimates that it would be worth $40,000 today.

With his appetite whetted, Hugh didn't stop bartering there.

He traded managing an 1896 inn in North Carolina in exchange for a free place to stay for two years, during which he got to learn handyman skills that became useful later in life. He has also traded for clothes, trips, food, and art. Hugh estimates that over the years, he has traded for nearly $250,000 in goods and services.

His advice on bartering: Just ask! Don't be afraid to ask for anything, Hugh counsels. The worst that can happen is that you'll get a refusal. But in Hugh's experience, most of the time, people will say yes.

Here's to saying "Yes!" to barter.

GREAT TRADE!

Back in the day when Gary and Patty Myers of Olympia, Washington, had little ones running around the house, they longed for a night out. But finding a reliable babysitter was a chore, and paying for one just added to the financial strain of raising a young family, so the Myers family decided to form a babysitting cooperative. (They became so adept at running it that years later, Gary wrote an entire book about it: *Smart Mom's Baby-sitting Co-op Handbook.*)

Here's how they did it: They gathered together several moms who also had small children and were willing to trade babysitting duties. Each mom earned four points for each hour that she babysat. She got an extra two points an hour for each additional child that she minded. When a "sit" was complete, the moms reported the total points earned and spent to the co-op's "secretary."

The secretary's job was to take calls from the member moms (or dads, as the case may be) and connect them with other parents who were available. The secretary typically picked sitters who had few points saved up or were even in debt to the co-op. Usually the secretary would receive about two or three calls a week from members needing a sit, so the time commitment wasn't too large. The secretary would serve for about a month, and then the job would rotate to another parent in the co-op.

The group also had a member coordinator who was responsible for bringing new families into the exchange. The Myerses discovered that as children reached elementary-school age, the parents didn't need as many sits—partly because they could take the child with them to events and also because there were older siblings who were mature enough to do the job for free. So the member coordinator's job was focused on recruiting families with babies or preschoolers to keep the co-op active. Gary believes that co-ops function best when there are at least ten families involved. At that level, a mom can always count on a sitter being available.

The members would meet every third Monday of odd-numbered months to keep everything running smoothly, deal with any issues, and appoint new administrators. That schedule mostly avoided holidays, and since the meetings were child free and around eight o'clock in the evening, the moms could relax and enjoy a night out and each other's company.

TRADING TIP

When bartering with someone, try to bring as much value to the trade as possible. If you're trading your baby's outgrown clothes for an older child's clothing, throw in a used toy or two. Your barter partner will be thrilled and want to trade with you again in the future.

> **TRADING TIP**
>
> If the first time you approach someone about trading and he declines, don't give up. Wait a few weeks or months and then approach him again. His circumstances or opinion may have changed, and bartering might now be an option.

Talents, Skills, Hobbies, Gifts Quiz

Not sure what your talents or skills are? Take this quick quiz to assess yourself.

Do you like to do things with your hands, such as knitting, sewing, or refinishing furniture?

Are you mechanically inclined? Do you like working on automobiles, lawn mowers, or electronics?

Are you artistic? Do you like painting, drawing, or sculpting?

Are you sports minded? Do you like coaching and/or instructing?

Are you technology oriented? Like to work with hardware and/or software?

Are you into fashion? Do you like assembling outfits?

Do you like gardening? If yes, flowers or vegetables or both? Do you like doing yard work?

Do you like to write? Review items? Research?

Are you research oriented? Like to read and learn?

Do you love teaching, instructing? What are you an expert in or at?

Is decorating your passion? Colors, furniture, placement?

Are you musically inclined? Do you like to sing? Play the piano?

Are you skilled in office knowledge, like bookkeeping, database management?

Do you enjoy graphic design? Marketing?

Do you love talking to others? Are you a natural salesperson?

Ask for assessment assistance . . .

Ask friends and family what they see as your gifts and talents.

Ask coworkers.

Ask your pastor, rabbi, or spiritual mentor.

Ask your cochair on a committee.

Think about a time when someone complimented you on something you did, even if it was long ago.

WORKSHEET

My personal list of gifts and strengths:

Gifts, talents, strengths my family and friends see in me:

My degree(s), training are:

In my past careers I have done:

In my current career I have done:

My true passion is:

Here are some ways I could barter these talents, skills, hobbies, and gifts:

CHAPTER 4

TRADING IN THE FAST LANE

If I had my life to live all over again, I would elect to be a trader of goods rather than a student of science. I think barter is a noble thing.

—Albert Einstein

If you want to speed up the whole barter–transaction dating dance (or avoid it entirely), you should enroll in a trade exchange. Commercial barter exchanges have been around in the United States since 1954 and are dedicated solely to making barter happen efficiently. See the Resources section for more listings of barter exchanges, or visit the Web sites of the International Reciprocal Trade Association (www .irta.com) and the National Association of Trade Exchanges (www.natebarter.com).

Barter exchanges are membership-based, for-profit companies that broker trades between a wide range of small, medium, and large businesses. While exchanges are primarily focused on serving companies, many welcome individuals with one caveat: They have to be able to trade a steady stream of goods or services or make a one-time trade that is lucrative enough to make up for the fees required with membership. If you have one item that you want to trade and don't expect to barter any others for quite some time, a barter exchange isn't right for you, with a couple of exceptions we discuss below. Every exchange charges monthly fees, and if you aren't trading fairly frequently, the fee will make the membership too costly for you. In those cases, trading on free Web sites like U-Exchange and BarterQuest is a better choice than using a commercial exchange.

Now, having noted that you'll need to have a steady stream of trades on an exchange, there can be exceptions to this rule. If you have an item that is worth big bucks, then it's time to chat with an exchange broker or owner to see what you can work out. A piece of land, a vintage automobile, or high-end jewelry might be enough to earn you a short-term entry to an exchange. Some exchanges will sign up a member who has a seasonal or limited-availability item because it's appealing to the members and helps the exchange owner provide a special treat that enhances the value of the exchange to the members.

During the summer, Maurya Lane, owner of Barter Business Exchange in Cary, North Carolina, allows an area farmer to offer his blueberries to her members. The farmer pays the exchange's monthly fee during the period in which he participates, which makes being a member affordable for him. The lesson here is that if you've got a hot item or one in limited supply, ask the exchange owner or the broker for a break on the monthly fee. You'll have more luck with this strategy if the exchange is locally owned rather than one of the large national chains, such as ITEX. National exchanges may allow for individual traders, and it never hurts to ask. The best time to do this is a month before you anticipate that people will want your product or service if there is any seasonality to it. You might have several cords of firewood ready to go right before summer, but hardly anyone is going to be interested in burning a fire just ahead of the hottest time of the year. But by early September, you'll be in a much better position to negotiate a limited-exchange membership as the weather cools and the first autumn leaves begin drifting toward the ground.

Keep in mind the value of what you have to swap, as you'll need to factor that into your finances as well. In addition to the sign-up and monthly maintenance fees, barter exchanges also charge their members a percentage of the value of each transaction they make. The one-time sign-up fee ranges from zero to $500 and is often a combination of cash and trade credits. For example, you might pay $250 in cash and $250 in a barter debit to start out. The monthly maintenance fee is typically $10 to $15 cash and an equal amount of trade debits. Generally speaking, the percentage charged for each transaction ranges between 10 percent and 15 percent of the value of the deal. The transaction fee is paid in cash, and who pays it depends on the exchange. Some charge each partner an equal percentage of the deal; others charge just the buyer of the good or service. If you pay cash for a portion of the item's price, you won't have to pay a transaction fee on that part.

The most important thing is to ask about all the fees the exchange charges before you sign up. You should have a clear picture of how much cash you'll need to do business. Barter won't be your friend if you go into the red trying to trade your stuff. You'll need to consider those costs and whether you think you can recoup them over time or whether you simply don't have enough cash to get started. Since so many exchanges accept the membership fee in cash and trade credits, that helps to reduce your cash outlay. Of course, for locally owned exchanges, it never hurts to ask that the fee be waived or paid entirely in barter since you're an individual rather than a business. Ask to pay for your monthly mainte-nance fee in barter as well, since you're not a large business and don't have the cash flow businesses have.

When you are evaluating an exchange, you must do some essential research before you sign on the dotted line. Your first call or Web site visit should be to your local Better Busi-ness Bureau to check out the exchange's standing. It also helps to see if the exchange is in good standing with one of two associations that exchanges typically belong to: the Inter-national Reciprocal Trade Association (IRTA) or the National Association of Trade Exchanges (NATE). If the exchange isn't a member of these two associations, we make a policy of not doing business with them. We also recommend that you deal with exchanges (or brokerages) that are well established and have a good reputation in the community. That isn't to say a newcomer won't be a good bet; everyone has to get started somewhere. But some exchanges start and fold quickly if there is too much competition, their policies are too restrictive, or they are trying to cover a geographic area that is too broad. If an exchange folds while you have credits outstanding, you will have lost the trade dollars as well as the fees you've paid in cash and trade. Sadly, there are disrepu-table businesspeople everywhere, but you can protect your-self just by doing a bit of research ahead of time.

After you've gotten a thorough understanding of the brokerage's fees, ask to see a list of its members. Evaluate the list to see if there are enough businesses to offer you the products and services that you want. If you don't find enough of what you want, that particular exchange probably isn't going to be worth the fees required. If you find a satisfying number of potential trading partners, consider whether you'll be able to use those goods or services often enough to make the exchange a benefit for you. Building up trade credits won't do you much good if you can't find partners to spend them with. You also won't have maximized your membership and may have to put it on hold until more and varied members join. An on-hold membership will still cost you monthly fees without bringing any goodies into your household. Ask how many members have accounts on hold. Their names may appear on the membership list, but if their account is on hold, you won't be able to barter for their goods or services. If the number seems high—say, 30 percent or more—that's another red flag.

Take down the names and phone numbers of three or four members who haven't provided testimonials to the exchange. Make a quick call to them and ask if they are happy with their experience. Ask the following questions:

- Does the exchange respond to them promptly?
- What types of restrictions have they noticed on in-demand items?
- Do they find most of what they want?
- Is the exchange easy to work with?
- Are its policies understandable and fair?

If they respond negatively to any of these questions, and their explanations seem credible and raise concerns, this is probably not a good choice. Just be sure you don't rule out an exchange based on a single comment or one disgruntled member. If you do decide against a particular brokerage, many towns have more than one, and you may have a better choice available.

If the exchange representative won't show you a membership list, or they have only a limited list that seems skimpy, head for the exit. This is a sign that the exchange doesn't have a wide roster of companies to trade with or that many have left, dissatisfied. You should also be suspicious if the majority of the members are located in another state. Your chances of executing a successful deal are poor with so few trading partners at hand.

Check out the physical surroundings when you visit with the exchange representative. Are his or her offices dingy, disorganized, or lifeless? If the phones aren't ringing or all you see is a desk and chair, you may have wandered into a business that isn't really a going concern. You should expect to see activity, hear the phone ringing with members conducting business, and see computers running barter software to track trades. Minus those elements, alarm bells should sound.

The broker—the individual who will help you execute deals and serve as your primary contact for the exchange—is a key contact for you. Start by asking the broker a few pertinent questions. Ask how your broker is going to drum up business for you within the exchange. And don't just ask what your exchange can do for you; be active in promoting your brokerage so that more people will join the exchange and provide you with additional trading opportunities.

Find out how many brokers the exchange has versus the number of members. A good rule of thumb is one broker for every 200 to 300 members. If there aren't enough brokers, you'll have a hard time connecting to make trades. Good exchanges have active brokers who are constantly looking to connect members with one another. Also ask if he or she has been certified as a trade broker by either the NATE or the IRTA see the Resources section for more information).

The exchange should also be publicizing what you and other members have to offer on a regular, easily accessible basis; that means a weekly (or more often) e-mail blast. Some exchanges will send out a regular "new member" announcement to churn up offers right away for the newbies. Even if you've been on the rolls for a while, make it a standard practice to call your broker regularly to see what's available. Brokers will have the most current information on what sort of barter inventory is at hand, including special one-time or limited-number items that many members will want. If you've built up a relationship with your broker, that special product or service might fall into your lap more often than if your broker can't quite seem to remember your name.

When Karen owned an exchange, she would regularly get limited offers like tickets to performances, vacation rentals, or a car. If the member was in good standing and had a strong barter history with her exchange, she would offer it to him or her first. Good standing equals being current on all cash fees that are owed to the exchange and having an excellent reputation for dealing well with your trading partners. In most cases, brokers will seek out those in good standing— their best customers—for special deals. These are typically members who have trade credits (rather than debts) on the books, keep in frequent contact with the broker, have no or few complaints against them, and are easy to do business with.

The other way to ensure that you get what you really want is to add your name to a waiting list for the specific items you need. When they become available, your broker will let you know. We've said it before, but it bears repeating: Barter is about building relationships.

To be really successful, don't leave all the promotion to your broker. You should take an active role in marketing yourself on the exchange. Attend membership events so that you can connect personally with others and—here's that phrase again—build relationships. Ask your broker if you can include a flyer about your goods or services in the exchange's next mailing. (Some exchanges will charge you for that service in barter dollars—any type of currency traded only through a barter organization.) The best part of that option is that you have to supply only the flyer; the exchange will take care of the stuffing and mailing. Or, if it's through e-mail, the exchange will handle sending the information to the entire membership.

Make sure you mention that you're a member of the exchange and looking for barter opportunities. Send out mass e-mails to the exchange's membership or call members individually to add that personal touch. Although you are a lone trader, you need to start seeing barter as a marketing tool for what you have to offer. Just remember to explain the benefits to the buyer rather than list the attributes of your product or service. Here's an example of a successful promo:

> *Keep your home's air clean with our eco-friendly soy candles. Buy one, get one free sale going on now!*

As opposed to this one:

> *Our candles use grade-A soy, the latest manufacturing technology, and extra-heavy-duty packaging that withstands U.S. Postal Service punishment.*

Which promo makes you want to buy those candles? See the difference?

Occasionally, you'll find that the item or service you need isn't offered by any members on the exchange. That doesn't mean you're out of luck and you have to break out your wallet. It's time to do a little legwork on your own. Call two or three companies or individuals who offer what you want.

Get bids from them as if you were a cash prospect. Then contact your broker and tell him you'd like to make a "trade purchase request." That's a form (see the Resources section for an example) that the broker will fill out that indicates what you're interested in and how much you would be willing to pay in barter credits for it.

Also, give the broker the names and contact information of the businesses you've already gotten bids from and the value of those bids. Tell him which one you would prefer and ask him to contact that business on your behalf about joining the exchange to make the deal on trade. You might think the broker would be aggravated to make a special effort for just one trade, but brokers are happy to do this sort of recruiting for you. After all, they get a big advantage when new members come aboard: Their existing member (you) is happy at finding a trading partner, the exchange gets its membership and monthly transaction fees from your deal and the future ones from the new member, and the rest of the membership gets access to the new company's products/ services. Everyone is happy.

When you trade, it's critical that your partner is ultimately satisfied with the deal. The truth is, you are conducting a business transaction. Just as in the cash world, if your partners aren't content with how you handled their deals, word will spread. Poor transactions will hurt your reputation, and you could find yourself with few or perhaps no trades while still having to pay your monthly fee. In the worst-case scenario, you could be kicked out of the exchange. On top of that, you'll have to contend with bad word of mouth spilling out of the exchange to the general community, especially if you live in a small town. Bottom line: Practice the Golden Rule and treat people the way you want to be treated.

A wonderful side benefit of giving good customer service to your barter partners is that they will refer you to non-barter customers; that means cash coming your way just from doing a great job at bartering. As we've said before, cash is king, and barter can lead you to more cash.

Another great advantage of being a member of an exchange is that you can get a barter loan to make purchases from members. The trick with using a barter line of credit is making sure you can do enough trades to "pay back" your credit line. Ask your broker to give you a report on your monthly trade credits so you can see what your trade flow is. Also be aware that some brokerages will charge you interest on the line, typically 0.5 percent to 1 percent a month (depending on the policy of the exchange). That's a high rate of interest that has to be repaid in trade and should not be ignored.

TRADING LIGHTLY

If you don't have a regular stream of products or services to sell on an exchange, there is still another option open to you—the subaccount. A full member of an exchange can add a secondary, or "subaccount," to his or her membership. The subaccount can sell to the main account. The main account will pay for the joining fee, which is reduced because of being a subaccount, and will be responsible for the transaction fees on the sub's trades. The difference is that the subaccount can't earn barter credits for selling items to other members. You can earn credits only by selling to the main account. As a sub you'll be able to spend the credits you earned with anyone else on the exchange.

Suppose you do upholstery as a hobby, and a restaurant owner wants you to repair her seats. You can become a subaccount of the restaurant, perform the work, and receive the barter credits. Then you can spend those credits for anything another member is offering: dentistry, lawn care, tools, and so on.

Subaccounts are best suited to one-time trades (bartering a boat, plane, car, or home) or when you are a repeat supplier to a main account, such as a janitorial service. To get started as a subaccount, you'll need to contact an exchange member and propose the deal. The member will then work out the details with the exchange.

OFF-THE-GRID TRADING

While trade exchanges are great, we recognize they aren't for everyone. If you have a low-volume trading capacity or ability or don't want to put yourself at risk of the cash and tax burden involved in exchange trades, there are other options.

In some communities, grassroots groups have started their own barter exchanges that have very low or no fees attached. These are homegrown efforts that are aimed at helping individuals trade to relieve their financial pressures. They can be very informal groups that have something in common, such as stay-at-home moms or guys who love choppers. Barter is just one of the benefits of belonging to the group. In other instances, these are mini exchanges devoted to enabling trade among individuals or microbusinesses.

Sometimes these exchanges are limited to one city; in other cases they cover an entire state. This is a great way to get started doing direct trades. You won't have the fees associated with commercial barter brokerages or the pressure to trade at a high volume to make those fees worthwhile. You'll still be able to build community. Just make sure to get a handle on whether there are a sufficient number of traders in your area to justify joining the group. That's especially true if you have a large number of items that would be too heavy or bulky to mail affordably. If the group is just getting started, talk to the organizer about what his or her plans are to promote it so that the exchange will attract more traders.

Having a Web site without any plan to get the word out about the brokerage could mean that expansion will be slow, and you might have fewer items to choose from during that period of growing pains.

So how do you find grassroots barter exchanges? Search for them on the Internet and see the Resources section in this book for a listing. Look for postings on community bulletin boards. Search Meetup.com, which has a large number of formal and informal bartering groups. You might even call your local commercial barter exchange and explain that you're not ready to join yet. Ask if it can recommend a local group where you can learn the ways of trading. Wise brokers will recognize that as you develop a better understanding of barter, you might one day reach a level at which it would make sense to join their brokerage.

TIME BANKS

One of the most exciting barter options available is the "time bank." Community groups, nonprofit organizations, governments, and others have created time banks, particularly to help low-income or cash-poor residents in their towns. As part of the social justice or poverty eradication movement, Dr. Edgar S. Cahn, cofounder of the National Legal Services Program, conceived the concept of time banks in 1980. He was searching for a solution to drastic cuts in government social services.

A time bank is a system that allows each member to provide a good or service to earn a credit. Often these credits are called "hours," and most often, they are equal to an hour of the member's labor providing a service such as plumbing, sewing, child care, or volunteer work. But an hour can also equal the value of a good the bank's store has in stock or the number of hours a member required to produce a good. Each time bank determines the value of its own currency. So, for example, if you drove a neighbor to and from the doctor, you would earn an hour from the time bank you are both members of. The member who receives the service reports the credit to the time bank, where an account for both is maintained and tracked.

Members of the bank work for an hour, providing whatever skill or talent they have. It could be as elaborate as electrical work or as informal as babysitting or driving a disabled person to the grocery store. Sometimes the time dollar is earned just by going to a movie with an elderly person. The trades aren't necessarily direct, since time dollars earned can be spent with any other member.

Time banks are especially good at helping low-income individuals who need access to more resources than they have the cash for, but they are also meant to help people who may be lonely and want companionship, as well as the opportunity to be involved in their communities, such as seniors or the disabled. Time banks are often an altruistic system that helps even the playing field for anyone who is a member. If you are a plumber, an hour of your time is equal to an hour of time ironing clothes for someone. Besides services, some community organizations have also created "time dollar stores," in which people can spend their time dollars on essential goods such as toothpaste, toilet paper, diapers, and so on.

Organizations set up time banks as a way of providing resources to a community that has few. These groups, often social service organizations, also hope to strengthen communities so they can tackle issues that affect them, as well as encourage relationships in which people will help one another rather than remain uninvolved strangers. Time banks are particularly helpful when there is a recession, there are few jobs, or economic difficulty is beating down the community.

Formal time banks typically require grants or cash infusions to pay for software and other supplies to manage the system. They also need an administrator to keep up with hours worked and redeemed as well as any problems that arise. If you are considering starting a small-scale time bank, it certainly can be managed with a home computer and a few hours of time each week. To find out more about how to operate a time bank, visit www.timebanks.org.

Another flexible system has developed around barter systems. Pioneered by community organizer Paul Glover, people in Ithaca, New York, created their own barter system. Members of Ithaca Hours, as it's called, earn one Ithaca Hour for every $10 in value for goods they sell or services they provide to other members of the exchange. The exchange issues its own perfectly legal currency, or scrip, in increments of one hour or fractions of hours. The system, which started in 1991, had hundreds of business members and thousands of individual members at its peak. People trade conventional goods and services such as handicrafts, electrical work, acupuncture, and tax preparation with individuals and businesses. Businesses sell a wide range of items, often for a combination of cash and scrip. Members can trade freely with anyone else in the system just as they would spend or receive cash.

But members were quite creative as well. One gentleman sold meteorites he discovered to other meteorite collectors. Another member earned Ithaca Hours for removing a television set for a family who wanted to limit the amount of TV their kids were watching. Some parents pay their children's allowance in Ithaca Hours currency.

If your town doesn't have a barter community like this, you could be bold and start one yourself. The key is to have a paid facilitator manage the system so that it runs smoothly. Here are some other things to consider:

- Have an attractive currency that is difficult to counterfeit.
- Spread the membership far and wide.
- Publicize the system's offerings through a variety of methods besides just a membership directory.
- Make the scrip easy to use.
- Conduct operations honestly and openly.
- Pay your administrator(s) less than 5 percent of the total value of currency in circulation, or you'll risk inflation.
- Promote the use of the system as a way to encourage community pride and interaction.

The results of time banks and community barter networks are impressive. Not only do people keep more of their scarce cash, but they also build stronger ties to one another that help them solve problems, get along more congenially, reduce political fighting, enhance compassion and understanding, and generally strengthen the community. Glover witnessed better relations emerge between normally combative groups and individuals because they had interacted with Ithaca Hours.

If a time bank or barter network doesn't exist in your town and seems too daunting an endeavor to launch, look for specialized networks. Many neighborhoods have swap meets, babysitting co-ops, cookie exchanges (especially around the Christmas holiday), dinner exchanges, seed swaps, clothing swaps, livestock swaps, and more. Let necessity be your inspiration. If there is something you need, chances are there is a fair number of other people in your community who need it as well and would be willing to work together to set up a barter network. You are limited only by the time you are willing to invest and your own imagination.

GREAT TRADE!

As college student, Jonathan Marsh walked into the Tucson office of BXI, a national barter exchange, with an enticing proposal: He offered to barter stereo systems. Co-owners Terry and Lee Brandfass were surprised that someone so young was approaching them to barter such a desirable item. They decided to take Jon on as a barter member because they thought it would be fun to have a young student in the exchange. Besides, they didn't have a stereo system dealer at that time and felt like the membership would be a good real-world learning opportunity for the business major.

The Brandfasses provided Jon with a $600 credit for stereos he purchased and then sold on the exchange. With those in hand, he started trading right away. He used some of his credits at restaurants near the University of Arizona and then expanded his business to include office supplies and printing, which earned him even more barter credits. As the enterprising student approached graduation, this experience helped him open his first business—selling stereo equipment. He joined the exchange as a business member and traded for many years in Tucson.

Later Jon moved to Phoenix and started MistAMERICA, a company that creates mist and fog systems for outdoor pools and other areas. He joined BXI in Phoenix as well and has bartered repeatedly for his business and personal use. Besides giving his company an edge over his competition, Jon has also enriched his personal life by bartering through BXI.

TRADING TIP

If you don't expect to do enough trades to join a barter exchange, look for businesses that display a trade exchange emblem (such as ITEX) on their doors or in their sales materials. This tells you that the owners and managers are quite familiar with barter and might be willing to consider a direct trade with you.

CHAPTER 5

THE UPSIDES AND DOWNSIDES OF BARTER

There's no doubt that we're huge fans of barter (not that you were wondering), and we certainly believe there are more reasons to barter than not. But we are also advocates for empowering you to be an informed trader so that you have a full command of using barter as a tool that will enhance your life, not hurt it. So as much as we love the upside of barter, we also want to explain the downsides so that you'll have a clear picture of how to extract as much good from it as you can. Here are some awesome positives and cautionary negatives to consider.

We'll start with the positives.

UPSIDES

As we mentioned earlier, there are many excellent reasons to barter: to save cash, to acquire more goods and services that you wouldn't have had otherwise, and to reduce the panic that comes from a low- or no-wage life, just to name a few. But there are some other excellent reasons to barter that you might not have considered.

When you start whittling away at the stuff cluttering your garage, attic, closets, shed, doghouse, and so on, you are not only creating barter opportunities but also simplifying your life. Simplifying and cleaning out the extraneous can launch a wonderful barter life because you will be making room for all of the great new stuff you'll acquire through trade. Besides giving you more living space by reducing the number of objects in your home, you'll also get a mental boost out of less clutter. It's pretty much the same as that great feeling you get when you plop down on the couch after having just cleaned your home, banishing all those knickknacks to their proper space. Some people we know say that reducing clutter makes them more productive because they feel like they've expanded the space around them and eliminated objects/ projects that were generating guilt, which, in turn, gener-ated more creative ideas and improved their problem-solving skills. At a minimum, reducing clutter just makes them feel so much lighter and better.

Barter also teaches you invaluable negotiating skills. If you think only in terms of plunking down your dollars and getting what you want, barter will teach you to really think about the value of an object or service and how much you want to invest in having it. Since prices aren't always fixed, you simply have to negotiate. This isn't an adrenaline-charged haggle like what you experience when you bargain for a new car. Rather, barter is more of a chat-over-the-back-fence type of transac-tion between two friendly folks. If the goodwill falls away, the deal typically falls apart. So while you're learning those valu-able negotiation skills, you also get a few lessons in human relations that they didn't teach you in high school or college.

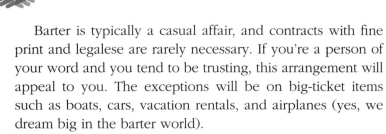

Barter is typically a casual affair, and contracts with fine print and legalese are rarely necessary. If you're a person of your word and you tend to be trusting, this arrangement will appeal to you. The exceptions will be on big-ticket items such as boats, cars, vacation rentals, and airplanes (yes, we dream big in the barter world).

If you're a budding artist, career changer, or student, barter can help you build a portfolio of work that can land you more jobs and lead to a more robust résumé. While you could offer to provide your services for free, barter ensures that what you are providing is more highly valued because the buyer is giving you something in exchange rather than just getting something for nothing.

Chicago artist J. S. G. Boggs is a great example. Boggs was having a coffee in a restaurant when he doodled a one-dollar bill on his napkin. The server was so enchanted by his drawing that she asked if he would like to pay for his ninety-cent coffee with the drawing. From that point on, Boggs began drawing banknotes from around the world and offering to barter them for restaurant meals or other goods. He refuses to sell his currency drawings for cash, saying that their creation and barter is a form of performance art. Collectors now clamor for his bills, and they have to track his movements so that they can offer cash to the person who received them. Some have even hired private investigators to track down the art if it changed hands multiple times. When gallery owners resell his work, they will often get far more than the face value of the "currency." A Boggs dollar can go for 500 real dollars (or more) on domestic and international markets. Besides being a talented artist, Boggs has generated publicity and made a name for himself simply because of the way he places his art into the marketplace.

Imagine if Boggs had simply tried to sell his work in galleries or at shows; would people have understood what he was doing? Would it have been nearly as interesting and desirable without the barter element? Because Boggs bartered, he generated a demand for his work and put it into many more hands than if it was hanging, unpurchased, in a gallery. Boggs owes his success in no small part to barter.

The end result for people who are able to trade their creations for something they want is a boost in self-esteem and pride in their work. That's no minor accomplishment in today's demanding, competitive world, where artists struggle to be noticed. After all, there are only so many places for a musician to play, an artist to display a painting, or an actor to ply her craft. Barter offers another route besides "getting paid" to bank some improved self-esteem and a richer sense of the value of your talents.

An added bonus of trading the works of your own hands to a larger audience is simply the sense of accomplishment you get. You're telling the world, "Hey, look what I did! And somebody else loved it enough to give me something valuable for it."

When you barter your arts or crafts, you've cleaned out space for your next project. Moving your "inventory" also gives you the perfect excuse to buy more raw materials to make new creations. Besides, your significant other will love you more. Why? Because you saved money by bartering to feed your habit. If people are wearing, displaying, or otherwise making others aware of your talents, you could pick up some additional barter partners and even some cash customers who became aware of your craft because your barter partner displayed it. Now you can see the exponential power of barter.

Texas artist Pablo Solomon is a great example. Although Pablo is a gifted painter and sculptor, people don't always want to spend a great deal of cash on his art, or in tough economic times, they aren't able to pay for a piece. That hasn't slowed Pablo down. Ever since he was a kid growing up in a poor family, Pablo and his family have bartered. When he was a little boy, he and his dad would play "beat the garbage truck" in order to grab the great castoffs people had tossed to the curb before the garbagemen came to cart them away. Then they would fix up the newfound "trash" if necessary and trade it for things they needed. Barter was just a way of life.

Over the years Pablo has traded a Ford Bronco for a heating and air-conditioning system. When the system needed repairs fifteen years later, he traded a Navajo rug to the technician who overhauled it. He has traded antiques for lavish diamond jewelry for his astonished wife and muse, Beverly, who didn't know anything about barter until they got married.

Pablo is resourceful, too. When his buddy who runs the cement plant dredges the river and comes up with arrowheads from the sand, he calls Pablo. Pablo trades him antique bottles that he's always on the lookout for because he knows his buddy loves them.

Barter has been the biggest help to Pablo's career. As he's become more established in the art world, Pablo will occasionally trade his artwork to a client. Sometimes it's a pure trade; other times it's a combination of cash and trade. Once a customer came to Pablo and asked him to sculpt an image of her from her days as a ballerina. They agreed that she would pay for the sculpture with a combination of cash and barter. After Pablo had finished the piece and the woman and her husband had put it on display in their home, they flew Pablo and Beverly on a private plane to their mansion. Pablo and Beverly landed at their private airstrip and joined the couple at a lavish party to celebrate the sculpture and Pablo. There were lots of well-heeled folk at the party, and Pablo and Beverly had a great time meeting them and showing off Pablo's art.

A few days later, several of the partygoers began calling Pablo to buy other pieces of his art, and they all paid in cash. Because Pablo bartered, he was able to expose a lot more people to his sculpture and, in turn, sell more art for cash. At the same time, he was helping to spread his reputation as a quality artist, and his career has developed serious momentum in the years since. For Pablo, barter has evolved from a means of surviving to a means of thriving.

The more trading partners you have, the more you can extend your contacts. And the more contacts you have, the more referrals or repeat trades you'll get—including maybe even some cash buyers as well. If you track your trades as we recommend, you'll develop a growing database or phone list of people whom you can contact for even more barter. These are people who are already barterers, so you can contact them first when you have items to trade, which could speed up your transactions. All of these partners can then connect you to their friends and family, personally recommending you as a reputable trader; they can let people know what you have or put the word out about what you're looking for. Maybe you'll even meet your next sweetie pie through barter (which is a friendly business, after all).

Barter also has time power. By that we mean you can use barter to leverage your stuff or skills to get services that save you time. Wouldn't it be a joy to have someone clean your house, wash your car or dog, mow your yard, or cook your dinner? Most likely, you'll be trading your own labor to receive these sorts of services continuously. But the best part of this is that you get to trade a chore for doing something you love. It can have the added benefit of reducing your stress level because you don't have to do it all. Finally, you've got help, and you can enjoy life a little bit more.

Maybe the biggest positive of barter is the psychological component: Once you start bartering, you'll never again think

of yourself as being broke. As long as you've got something you can offer in trade, you'll be able to get something that you were spending cash on before. That means you have an ongoing way of keeping cash in your pocket, saving you from the depression and the limited thinking that goes along with a "tapped-out" mind-set. And since barter is a looser, freer form of exchange, you don't always need to have exactly the cash value of what you want. If you work as an electrician, you get paid your hourly rate, and the only way you'll make more is by working extra hours. But when you're trading your electrical skills, you choose which jobs to take and how many hours you'll work depending on what the other person has to offer. If you get the work done faster, you still get what you're trading for. In your day job, if you complete the work more quickly, chances are good you'll just get assigned more work for the same amount of pay. The concept of an hourly rate can become much more fluid and work in your favor when you barter.

DOWNSIDES

So that we don't fall into the Pollyanna category, we definitely want to explain the downsides of barter. Few of them are deal killers; they are just cautionary notes that you should be aware of so that you can be a savvy trader. Some of them you'll be able to avoid just because you are aware of them. Others will feel less bothersome because you are prepared for the experience.

First and foremost on the list is patience. Cash is harder to earn and easier to spend; barter is easier to get and harder to spend. Since barter isn't as liquid as cash, deals take longer to find, set up, and execute. Barter is like dating: You have to find where the type of girls or guys you like hang out, figure out who is a good match for you and who feels the same about you, and then make him or her a proposition (ahem—not to take the analogy too far). Since this process generally takes longer than paying cash, you'll have to develop patience. If you aren't a naturally patient person, this will be a great opportunity to work on developing that skill. (You don't have to like it, and you can even grit your teeth while it happens if that makes you feel better.) If you build more time into your thinking right from the start, barter will be less trying for you. The scramble to find a trading partner is less arduous if you plan ahead to acquire the items you want. If you know that the kids are going to need new jeans in a few months, start looking for a trade before they're bursting the seams.

Another downside: taxes. If you are a high-volume trader or your trades are directly related to how you earn your paycheck, Uncle Sam wants to get to know you better. You'll owe taxes on the value of all your trades, and the Internal Revenue Service doesn't have a sense of humor about these things. You'll have to pay to play. The same philosophy applies to barter exchanges. A fee will apply to every trade you make, and you need to budget for those cash outlays along with your monthly fees. Remember: The fees can range from 5 percent to 12 percent of the total value of the item or service bartered depending on the exchange.

Some deals will be inconvenient. You might have to drive farther, ship goods across the country, shop in the off-hours or at a less-desirable location, or purchase second-run or off-season inventory. The smaller the profit margin on an item or the higher the demand for it, the more likely you are to be inconvenienced in acquiring it. Computers are one example. The markup on them is low, and they are always in demand. You probably won't be able to get the state-of-the-art machine you heart desires, but you'll still get a spiffy computer.

Also be aware that not everything you want will be available when you desire it. Restaurants may not allow you to

use barter cards or scrip, an exchange's currency, during prime dining hours on Friday and Saturday nights. A vacation rental home in Florida might be unavailable in the middle of winter. Retailers might allow you to acquire only off-season inventory. If you're a member of an exchange, sometimes what you want isn't offered by any of the members. You'll have to be a bit intrepid and find a nonmember who can be invited by the exchange to join and trade with you. Since business owners are just like consumers, they have to be educated about barter. In the process, they may take their sweet time joining up or decide it's not in their best interest (a decision we would argue strongly against in most cases, of course). All of that combines to place limits on your ability to barter—at least temporarily. One solution is to approach a different vendor about making a trade. That company might be more open-minded, and you'll be back in the game.

You may also find that discounts, coupons, sales, or other promotions aren't available for barter deals. In other cases, you may still be able to get the advertised discount, but it won't be as generous as the one given to cash customers. The problem is that some retailers and service providers don't view barter customers in the same way as their cash clients, which is a shame in our opinion. But keep in mind that business owners who resist offering discounts coupled with barter need to retain a certain amount of cash to keep operating, which explains why they may not be able to honor discounts. You can still point out that value is exchanging hands in both cases; only the form of compensation is changing. That's the argument we would recommend making to those vendors (in a pleasant way, of course), along with the idea that as a happy customer, you'll be excited to spread the good word about the business. The worst thing that can happen is that you still won't get the promotion, but at least you tried.

In a similar vein, you may find that trade partners don't give you the same top-drawer treatment that they provide their cash buyers. You may not notice it at first, but if you trade repeatedly with the seller, you might eventually see the differences. Maybe you get the least-desirable table at the restaurant, or the higher-grade model is rarely available when you want it. Don't get your dander up. The best approach is to bring the discrepancy to the seller's attention and ask him how he would like to remedy the situation. Explain that since you are giving him excellent treatment and would like to be a great word-of-mouth promoter for the business, you would like to be treated the same as his wallet-packing customers. If you still aren't satisfied, look for another trading partner and move on.

Perhaps you're the one giving poor customer service. You might be thinking that barter isn't cash, and everyone knows that they won't get the same attention in a trade as they would in a cash deal. You'd be wrong. And you could be damaging your little enterprise, even if it's just a sideline. Your good name will also get hit with a big mud ball, and don't assume that because you live in a big city that people won't know. People talk and bad news travels fast, especially if your trades are interrelated with other direct barter partners like a babysitting co-op.

While you are entitled to the same level of customer service as a cash customer, it's important to recognize that trades are often unbalanced in favor of one partner over the other. Unequal trades are simply the nature of barter. The trick is to make sure that they aren't grossly skewed. Some traders will overvalue their item and try to inflate the trade to receive more on their end. In other instances, the seller is simply a higher-price vendor whose cost is justified because of quality or some other component.

Karen once used a printer for a project who would only make the trade for a combination of barter credits and cash. Later Karen discovered that she could have had the entire job done through another printer for the same amount of trade dollars that she had paid in cash. If Karen had gotten bids from other printers, she would have realized that she could have bargained for a better deal. Do the research on prices or get other quotes so you can avoid paying more than you have to.

Trades that take place over a period of time or repeatedly between the same partners tend to start out more equal than not and then begin to favor one partner as the traders get to know one another and relax. The adage "familiarity breeds contempt" applies here, at least to a small degree. To avoid that sort of imbalance in a prolonged transaction, have a plan that both partners must agree to stick to for a certain period of time. If the trades have gotten too lax by the end of the period, that's the moment to take stock and renegotiate or to remind your partner about the original agreement. As long as you still feel like you're getting a decent deal, go forward. If you're coming out on the short end, you can try to negotiate a little sweetener. If you have a decorator who is redesigning a room for you, and you feel like what you are offering is of greater value, ask her if she would decorate another room to make up the difference. This is where knowing the market value of the trade is helpful. If you can demonstrate that your item or service is worth more than hers on the open market, you've got a stronger chance of success. If your trading partner isn't willing to ante up a little more, perhaps you can scale back your offering in quantity or quality. You can also ask for cash (or offer it, if the shortfall is yours) to even it out. If that still doesn't work, you have to ask yourself if having the item or service is worth a bit of inequity rather than having to hand over greenbacks.

A perfect example is our friend Kyle MacDonald. You might have heard of Kyle, the enterprising Canadian who wanted a house but didn't have the money for it. He created a blog about his situation and offered to barter one red paper clip in exchange for something more valuable. He planned to trade each item he received for something more valuable still as he bartered his way to a house. (You can read more about Kyle in this chapter's Great Trade! story.)

The first trade Kyle made was for a doorknob. Clearly swapping a red paper clip for, in this case, an artistic hand-made doorknob was an unequal trade. But what was working in Kyle's favor was the earnestness and sense of humor he applied to his cause and the fact that he was generating buzz around it through his blog posts. Kyle's style was simply to be open to all comers and see what emerged—fair or not. And that's what moved him progressively forward toward his goal. As he says, barter sometimes allows one person to get a great deal for very little input.

Another downside is overenthusiasm. Some folks get so excited in the hunt for the deal that they trade for things they don't really need or want. We understand how exciting it is to find a great barter partner, but you should ask yourself in each transaction if you really want what you're being offered. A trade may seem like getting something for nothing, but what you're selling has value, including trades that involve your labor rather than goods. Once you've traded it, you'll have only what you got in return. Will you be happy with it?

Of course, some barter deals don't get fulfilled as promised. It's a common occurrence. Our organic farmer friend Jacqueline Freeman once agreed to trade an old car that she and her husband no longer needed to a young woman in exchange for three cords of firewood. The woman and her boyfriend picked up the car and delivered two cords. They promised to bring the third cord soon. Jacqueline agreed that this would be fine. Ultimately, the young couple never returned with that third cord. Instead of being upset, Jacqueline laughed off the trade. While she would have liked to have the third cord of wood, she wasn't getting any use out of the car and was glad to have it off her property. She and her husband greatly enjoyed the firewood they did receive, and, in the end, she felt like the trade mostly worked out.

It helps to have a flexible attitude about barter. If you're a by-the-book sort of person, you'll wind up aggravated and aggrieved on some trades. Save yourself the stress and years off your life by looking at the big picture and recognizing that barter, even when it's imperfect, is usually beneficial.

Some deals look promising and then fall through after lengthy negotiations or at the last minute. As frustrating as that is, you can let the deal rest for a while and then try again. This is a lot easier to do if you keep the tone friendly throughout. You never know what might be going on in someone's personal life that makes a trade too hard to do at that moment. If you're the one who gets cold feet about a trade after you've already shaken hands on the deal, you really should go through with it unless you have a stellar reason for not doing so. "But I never signed a contract with anyone," you might argue. Contracts are rarely a big part of casual bartering, which is a positive as well as a negative. But don't be fooled: Even if you didn't sign a written contract, a verbal agreement or e-mail can be just as binding. When lawyers or courts get involved, you'll be out of cash through legal fees or losing a case. You'll also have a damaged reputation and maybe even a scorched friendship if you were already buddies before everything went south. If you're part of an exchange or barter Web site, you could get the boot for bad behavior. Better to honor your words than to have to eat them.

Assertiveness is a key component of direct barter. The job of approaching a partner if you're not in an exchange or Web site, then negotiating, or handling deals gone askew, requires firmness and a measure of determination. If you're more shrinking violet than wheeler-dealer, you'll have to overcome your shyness to be successful. That's not an entirely bad thing. Consider how a bit more assertiveness would serve you well in the other areas of your life. And you won't have to pay to attend any self-esteem workshops or buy a single self-help book to develop that skill. (Besides, we'd just tell you to barter for the workshop or book anyway.)

Look at barter as a means to achieve multiple ends. You'll need to develop sales skills and approach the owner, top manager, or decision maker with your proposal. You may have to ask who that person is. You should start small with your first few trades so you can learn the process. Risk something nonessential and avoid becoming stressed because you desperately need to make the deal happen. Try Karen's tried-and-true approach: "This may be a crazy idea or a bit off the wall, but I have something I want to run past you. Would you be interested in trading X for Y?" In this unaggressive way, you give a prospective trader a chance to say no with grace or open a dialogue that has much less resistance around it.

Often, people will say "I don't think that's crazy at all." It's human nature not to attack or reject if you are being vulnerable. More often than not, Karen finds that this method works because it's simply less direct. Develop a method that works for you and just keep telling yourself, "The worst thing they can say is 'no.' "

So that's the best and worst of barter. We hope we haven't scared you off. Just realize that all of these things aren't guaranteed to happen at once. They are just part of the barter experience over the long haul. On balance, we have found barter to be a vastly more positive experience than a negative one. And we think you will too, if you keep the downsides in mind along with all the great bennies.

GREAT TRADE!

You may have heard about that guy who started with one red paper clip and traded until he acquired a house. That's Kyle MacDonald of Kipling, Saskatchewan, Canada. Kyle had an outrageous idea: Trade a common office supply for a new home. What we love about Kyle's story is that he was fearless, completely open-minded, and focused solely on barter. No cash was involved in these trades. Mostly, Kyle was trading to have fun, but he blogged about his entire experience, and having that Internet site helped generate a lot more offers and interest in the process. The turning point for him, which few traders ever experience, was when international media became intrigued with his audacious idea. Once he began getting media coverage, the value of his trades increased dramatically, moving him farther and faster toward his goal. His trades were crazy: an afternoon with rock star Alice Cooper, a movie role with actor Corbin Bernsen, and, finally, an entire house.

The most important part of the process for Kyle was just having fun. And he had lots of it (despite trading away the Instant Party kit, unused). Along the way he also learned much about barter, and he offers some tips:

- Don't trade for junk, and don't make any trades with anyone you don't trust.
- When you've got something to trade, talk it up among your friends, family, and maybe even a stranger or two.
- Post your offer on bulletin boards (Web and real); in e-mails; on CraigsList, your blog, or Web site; or anywhere else it might get noticed. For instance, if you've got a bike you want to barter, post your notice in a bicycle shop (with the manager's approval, of course).

- Finally, have fun with it all.

As Kyle noted, nearly all of the people he traded with came to his wedding several months later, and he still keeps in contact with them. For Kyle, barter is a party that never ends.

TRADING TIP

Got something awesome to trade that needs a special buyer? List it and its attributes at the bottom of your personal e-mail signature. Whoever you send mail to will see it, as will anyone it gets forwarded to. You could also try posting it on Listservs or forums that cater to people who adore your product or service.

TRADING TIP

Keep a list with you at all times of the items you'd like to have as well as the items you have to offer. That way, when someone is interested in the trade, you'll have your list ready to go and can start the discussion right away.

CHAPTER 6

THERE'S NO PLACE LIKE (SOMEONE ELSE'S) HOME

Trading goods and services offers some great, life-expanding potential for bartering fans. But your ability to barter doesn't end at your front door. That's just your jumping-off point for a special area of trade that can satisfy your travel lust or help you lay down roots in a new locale. Bartering for real estate opens up wide vistas of possibility. When we say *real estate*, we not only mean trading one house, a piece of land, or other property for another but also mean temporarily swapping your home with someone in a far-off land for a unique vacation. Real estate trades can also set you up in a time-share at the beach, in the mountains, in the middle of Manhattan, or by the shores of a windswept lake. There's no limit to where you can go with barter, and there are even opportunities for staying put once you get to your dream destination.

VACATION SWAPS

One of the most popular ways to save bundles of cash and provide you and your family with a whole different way of experiencing a new place or culture is trading your home with another family for a vacation. Multiple Web sites like HomeExchange.com allow travelers to find, scope out, and lock in vacation swaps with others all over the world. Got a hankering to spend a month in Paris? A week in Istanbul? A long weekend in Cancun? Here's your chance.

When you trade your home for someone else's, there are multiple benefits. The first and foremost is you save a huge sum of cash that you would have spent on a hotel or bed-and-breakfast. Think of all the wonderful ways you can spend that cash during your vacation other than just laying your head on a pillow. Have more luxurious dinners. Upgrade your flight to first class. Buy more or better souvenirs. Attend events like plays, games, or concerts you couldn't have otherwise afforded. Go on pricey excursions like skiing, parasailing, white-water rafting, swimming with the dolphins, spa visits, or high tea. The bottom line is you get to decide where to spend all of that now-available cash.

Another excellent advantage of staying in someone else's house, condo, or villa is that you will experience the place you traveled to in a more intimate way. Instead of staying in a tourist zone crammed with hotels and people selling you cheap tchotchkes, you will make your base of operations a home or apartment in a neighborhood (or a farm, ranch, or other interesting locale). You'll see how natives live, work, and play. You'll also have opportunities, if you want them, to get to know the neighbors and have a more personal interaction with them than you would typically experience in restaurants or hotels.

Early in her career when money was tight, Shera and her best friend, Johanna, traveled to Sydney, Australia, for a vacation. While dining in a restaurant on their first night in town, they began chatting with a vivacious couple intrigued by their American accents. When Joy and Brian discovered that Shera and her friend were visiting, they offered to let them stay at their condo in exchange for caring for their two cats while they went away for a long weekend. The couple lived just on the outskirts of Sydney in a lovely setting not far from a subway station. Joy and Brian could relax, knowing that their cats and home would be well cared for, gratis, while they were away. And Shera and Johanna had a great place to stay, saved a considerable amount on hotels, learned more about Australian culture than they could have imagined, and made friends they would never have met otherwise—all thanks to barter.

Making lifelong friendships is another benefit of home swaps. In the course of setting up your exchange, you'll correspond with your trading partners and get to know them fairly well. After all, you don't want to let complete strangers stay in your home, right? Those early relationships often continue to develop, especially if the two parties choose to swap vacation homes again.

That was definitely the case in the very first home swap for Suzanne and Wayne Horne. The Hornes traded their home in Phoenix for the home of a couple who lived outside London. Although that trade took place in 1975, the Hornes remained friends with their swap partners and cherished that friendship. Since then, they have traded homes in the United States as well as Paris; Prague; Edinburgh, Scotland; and Victoria, British Columbia, Canada. The Hornes correspond with their trading partners over several months, getting to know them and working out the details of the stay. Since they retired, the couple spends a month wherever they go and are often able

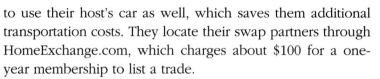

to use their host's car as well, which saves them additional transportation costs. They locate their swap partners through HomeExchange.com, which charges about $100 for a one-year membership to list a trade.

Home swapping can also extend to the use of a sailboat, RV, chalet, ranch, farm, or any other sort of trade, with the owners still involved and acting as hosts. One family gets a nice home away to visit and, in return, offers an exciting "experiential home visit." This is your chance to rope fillies on a dude ranch or track dolphins with marine biologists. Imagination and connecting with a trader are your only limits.

Another perk of a home trade is that you have access to the home's kitchen and can save money by preparing your own meals rather than eating out for the duration of your stay. You also get a bit more privacy than in a hotel, since various family members can divvy up the house's bedrooms for themselves.

So how does it work? The process is pretty simple. Before you get started, make a list of the destinations you'd like to visit and the times of year you'd like to go, as well as when your home will be available. The more flexible you are with your travel, the more likely it is you'll be able to make a successful exchange. Just don't book your transportation until you've got a confirmed agreement with another trader. Allow between four and six months to set up a trade. Sign up on a swap site and list your home, with lots of photos inside and out. Make sure you list the number of bedrooms, how many people it can accommodate, and any amenities that will make your home more attractive to potential traders. If you've got a gourmet kitchen, hot tub, pool, golf course, or gym at your disposal, those are important items to list. If your house is kid or baby friendly, especially if a crib is available, that's good information to provide as well. Give viewers an idea of how close you live to the area's main attractions and details about the transportation to those sights. If a car is available for their use, say so. Also specify smoking preferences and if animals live in the home, in case your visitors have allergies or don't want to care for a pet.

Expect to spend quite some time corresponding with your partners via e-mail, postal mail, and the phone to establish the ground rules of the trade. And you'll have to do quite a bit of preparation before you take off. That includes clearing out drawer, closet, pantry, and toiletry space for your guests. It's also essential that you provide a guide to the operation of your home, appliances, alarm, car, computers with passwords, emergency contacts, and other pertinent information to make their stay a success. Many swappers provide maps, tips on good restaurants, directions to sights, the nearest drugstore and grocery, and other helpful information. It's also a good idea to give them a phone number of a neighbor or relative who can help if they're in a jam and who have an extra set of keys to the home and car in case they get locked out.

Don't forget to indicate whether your guests are allowed to eat food that you've stored in your pantry, freezer, and refrigerator. If you have pets, you'll need to make sure that your guests are comfortable living with them and caring for them while you're gone. High-value items in your home are best stashed in a safe or safety deposit box or locked away in a room or closet that is off limits to the newcomers. Your home owner's insurance policy will cover any accidents your guests may have, so you don't need additional insurance for their stay. However, you should contact your auto insurer to make sure you are covered for driving their vehicle while you stay at their home, especially if they live overseas. You can ask that your guests do the same if they drive your car.

Once all the details are set, you're ready to book your flight and take off. You may get the opportunity to meet your hosts if your arrival or departures overlap. Often, though, you'll know each other only through e-mail and phone calls. In the end, the benefits of swapping homes will be worth the mystery of having friends you've never met stay in your home.

YOUR NEXT TEMPORARY HOME

Perhaps you've heard of those elusive people who somehow manage to live in a nice apartment or house for free (other than offspring, of course). How do they do that? Most of the time it's in exchange for being the resident manager or caretaker. That's just another form of barter and can be very helpful for cutting costs. If you have handyman skills, you're even more likely to snag a bartered residence since you can earn your "keep" through doing repairs and maintenance. But if you aren't handy around the house, don't despair. You can still barter.

Take our friends, Carrie and Steve: They sold their house and moved into the home of a colleague who had relocated to Florida but wasn't ready to sell his house in a depressed market. In exchange, Steve helped manage their friend's real estate business for about ten hours each week. At first, they had a handshake deal, but they eventually signed a lease with the owner to ensure there were no misunderstandings. Carrie and Steve paid the utilities, but they freed themselves from a mortgage while getting to live in a larger, nicer house than they had previously owned. They converted the money they were saving on mortgage payments into paying off debts, and they also invested in Carrie's life coaching business.

To get started, ask friends and family if they or anyone they know would be interested in trading rent for caretaking or some other service you can provide. If you don't have luck there, you can try CraigsList, or you can call property management companies, your local landlord association, real estate agents, and apartment complexes or residences with FOR RENT signs posted. While it might seem like a bold move to approach a property owner about bartered rent, the worst that can happen is that he or she will say "no." Trading your time or caretaking ability for a place to live can save you enormous amounts of money and stress and, for some people, from the prospect of being homeless. If you are able to work out a deal, you will save yourself thousands of dollars a year—money that you could save for a down payment on a house of your own, to pay off bills like Carrie and Steve did, to have a fabulous vacation, or to buy whatever is important to you.

TRADE THROUGH AN EXCHANGE

If your area is in the doldrums and real estate isn't selling well, you might consider selling your home through an online or commercial exchange.

First, the commercial exchange: You don't have to be a member of the brokerage initially to sell it, but you may have to join to be able to use your barter credits. Selling a home or property through an exchange is a fast way to move your property and get a large amount of trade credits that you can spend as you like. If you don't need that property, you could turn it into all manner of goods and services that you could use: chiropractic, gems, vacation time-shares, autos, massages, restaurants, home renovations—the list goes on and on. Just be sure you have a clear idea of how you want to spend all those trade dollars you are going to earn from the sale of your home. Otherwise, how will you know if the exchange can accommodate the purchases you want to make with tens of thousands of dollars in trade credits or cash?

Each brokerage will have different rules on how they conduct property barter, but many people will buy or sell for a combination of trade dollars and cash. If you are buying property through a commercial exchange, you will still need to obtain a mortgage; the good news is, you may be able to trade for your mortgage fees and other costs if the exchange has a lender member.

You can also trade other aspects of the transaction, such as a real estate agent or broker's commission; title insurance; closing costs; building, mold, and termite inspections; surveys; appraisals; attorney's fees; mortgage brokers; and more.

Some exchanges will issue a mortgage to their members for a property purchase. The member would still have to repay the mortgage and interest through trade dollars. The critical component in obtaining a mortgage on trade is making sure that you can earn enough trade credits to satisfy your monthly mortgage payments.

The good news is that although the trade exchange will issue a tax form indicating you had income from the sale of your property, you will be able to deduct the sale from your taxes just as you would normally, assuming that you bought a more expensive home in the same year.

THE 1031 EXCHANGE

There is yet another method of real estate barter, but this one allows you to defer paying taxes for quite some time. To execute this sort of transaction, you'll definitely need professional assistance.

For many years, farmers have been swapping land as their needs and commodities changed. In 1921, Congress enacted a law that allowed farmers to trade land without having to pay taxes on each swap. That law is the basis for a powerful tax deferral tool referred to as a 1031 exchange, tax-free exchange, or like-kind exchange.

A *1031 exchange* is best for property owners who are selling at a gain. (If you have a loss, it's not a good option because you'll want to deduct the loss from your taxes, not defer it.) A 1031 exchange doesn't apply to your home, or primary residence, or to people who are renovating or "flipping" houses as an investment for resale. However, 1031 exchanges are ideal for any type of real estate that is held for investment or business purposes. For example, most commercial, retail, industrial, residential rental, or vacant property may qualify for a 1031 exchange. Raw land or farmland may also qualify.

To get started, you'll need to contact a 1031 exchange facilitator, or "qualified intermediary." That's a company that can walk you through the steps of the deal and hold the cash from the transaction so you get the tax deferral. This type of firm must be contacted *before* closing in order to have the proper documents ready to make it a tax-deferred transaction. Trying to set up a 1031 exchange *after* a deal has closed is too late. To find these types of firms, contact the Federation of Exchange Accommodators (www.1031.org), the national trade association for these businesses.

The way it works is basically this: You agree to sell your property to a buyer, and your intermediary will accept the payment on your behalf. If your agent, attorney, or anyone else you have had control over in the prior two years accepts the payment for you, you could run afoul of the IRS rules and invalidate the 1031 exchange. You must choose a disinterested party. Since you'll be transferring that large payment to another person who will have total control over it, make sure you know the firm or individual well, or you will risk losing your money to a possible embezzler. It's best to deal with a well-established intermediary on the transaction. Since the intermediary will place the sales proceeds from the deal in escrow on your behalf, it is important to research the company's credentials. Check the company out with the Better Business Bureau. The following questions are good to ask the intermediary:

- How long has the company been in business as an intermediary?
- Do the owners have a tax or legal background?
- Will the firm set up separate accounts for each client (not mingle accounts or subaccounts)?
- What kinds of safeguards are in place to protect against fraud or stealing funds?
- Will your money be held in an account that is easily accessed yet still offers protection?
- Does the intermediary have adequate bond and insurance?

Once the funds have been transferred, you have forty-five days to notify your intermediary in writing of up to three "like" properties that you would prefer to purchase. If you had a storefront that you sold, you could designate another commercial property, vacant land that could be built upon, a vacation home, or residential rental property. At the same time, the clock starts ticking, and you have six months to purchase one of those three properties. If you fail to buy, you lose the option to defer the taxes. The key to deferring all the tax is to buy replacement property or properties that are equal to or greater than the sales price you received. If you buy property of lower value, you will pay tax on the difference. If you do make your planned purchase, you can defer the payment of federal capital gains tax, any applicable state taxes, and depreciation recapture tax (if applicable).

After owning the new property for a while, you could sell it and put those proceeds into another 1031 transaction and go through the process again. In that way, you would defer the taxes until eventually, you sell the "replacement" property and keep the cash. It is possible to eliminate tax payments by continuing to structure every sale as an exchange, continuously deferring the tax. After you die, your heirs receive the property at its current fair market value, and the previously deferred taxes are eliminated.

The intermediary who handles the payment and 1031 paperwork for you will likely charge you between $600 and $2,500 for his or her services. Some will charge a percentage of the sale price of the property. Clearly, this type of transaction isn't without cash costs. It's important to consult with your tax or legal advisor before entering into a 1031 exchange. The key to structuring a successful 1031 exchange is to plan ahead. Ideally, you should educate yourself before you sign a purchase or sale contract. Most intermediaries offer complimentary consultations or seminars to educate taxpayers on 1031 exchanges.

SWAPPING HOUSE FOR HOUSE

One other intriguing form of real estate barter exists, although it's rarer than most: the permanent house-for-house swap. In these trades, one home owner agrees to swap his or her home with another home owner. These trades can happen on the same street, same city, or across the country from each other. Web sites such as DomuSwap.com, U-Exchange.com, OnlineHouseTrading.com, and RealEstateExchange.com offer venues to connect with other potential swappers. Most charge a fee to list your home on their site, and there is no guarantee that you'll find a willing partner. One of the biggest advantages of swapping homes is that you don't need a real estate agent to handle the transaction. That means you'll also save the agent's commission, which can amount to tens of thousands of dollars depending on the value of your house.

Swapping homes can also give you an alternative to selling your property in a soft market.

In fact, swaps tend to work best if your real estate market is slightly sluggish. A deeply depressed market will make a swap partner much more difficult to find, in part because many people just need cash for their home and because housing prices are likely to have dropped dramatically, wiping out much of the value of the property.

By their nature, these swaps tend to be unequal. After all, no two existing homes are exactly alike. If one home is valued more than the other, cash or additional trades will have to change hands to even up the deal. You'll have all the same taxes, fees, and paperwork, such as a title search, surveys, inspections, and so on. You will also need to obtain a mortgage if you have to finance your side of the deal. But the good news is that mortgage lenders don't think of house barter any differently than a traditional mortgage.

Another critical component of house swaps is having equity in your home to begin with. Home owners who have little or no equity in their house are not good candidates for a swap unless they have a substantial amount of cash reserves to make a down payment on the new home. Ideally, both sellers want to have enough equity in their homes to cover a standard 20 percent down payment on the new home, plus closing costs.

Swaps are harder to execute, which explains why they don't happen every day. You have to think of a home swap as the simultaneous sale of two homes. That means, ideally, closing on the sale of both properties at the same time, even if the closings are in different locations. Simultaneous closings ensure that the buyer doesn't renege on the deal at the last minute, leaving you in the unenviable situation of having bought their home and failing to have sold yours.

The other aspect of a home swap that makes it more difficult is that you are most likely not going to find your dream house. Because so few people know about and are willing to swap homes, you have a limited pool of properties to choose from. That means some of the amenities you want, most in your next home may not be available in a swap. The house might be larger or smaller than you really want, in poorer condition than you desire, or in a neighborhood, or even a city, that isn't exactly where you wanted to live. You may fail to find any number of characteristics that you had on your new-home wish list. You have to determine how much you are willing to compromise to make a swap work. If you are inflexible and demanding, you are not a good candidate for a home barter. But if you are open to all comers and possibilities, you just might be able to seal the deal and line up the moving van.

GREAT TRADE!

When Sherry Crosslin and James Ray retired from their jobs as federal workers, they decided to pull up stakes and sell their home in Hampton, Virginia. But after their home was on the market for several months, they hadn't received any offers, and even interested lookers had stopped inquiring. After firing their third real estate agent, Sherry got busy and began looking for any way possible to find a buyer so they could realize their dream of moving to Las Vegas.

Sherry soon discovered DomuSwap, a home-swapping Web site. She listed their home and within a few months had found a buyer with a home in Thousand Oaks, California, who was interested in trading. Since the home wasn't too far from Vegas, they decided to trade. They agreed on a purchase price of $500,000 each for the houses and began writing up the paperwork with the help of their title companies and lenders.

When a bank appraised the home in California, the appraiser placed the value at $90,000 less than the price Sherry and James had agreed to. To make the deal work, the swap continued as planned by valuing both homes at $500,000, but to even out the trade a bit, Sherry and James provided the California buyer with cash to make up the lost equity in his home. Sherry conceded that although the California house wasn't her dream home, it enabled them to sell their property in Virginia and finally move to the West Coast to start the next phase of their lives.

TRADING TIP

Invite vacation swap guests to feel at home in your house so they have a great experience during the swap. Let neighbors know guests will be visiting so they can help put out the welcome mat while you're gone.

TRADING TIP

Leave a notebook with all the information your vacation swap guest will need to know about your home, vehicle, pets, appliances, area attractions, public transportation, emergency numbers, and other pertinent data that will make their stay a pleasure.

TRADING TIP

Before trying to sell your home through a barter exchange, review the membership rolls of the exchange and make a list, including dollar amounts, of goods and services you would like to purchase with the trade credits you'll earn. If there aren't enough members or items to spend your credits on, check out another exchange or ask the broker to recruit the type of business you want to buy from. If you still can't satisfy your wish list, selling through an exchange may not be right for you.

CHAPTER 7

BARTER, TAXES, AND YOU

When you earn a paycheck, you're not the least bit surprised that the Internal Revenue Service takes its chunk of taxes from your wages. Aggravating as that may be, it goes with the territory, and you know that's just part of the "cost" of working. But what about barter?

If you ask, plenty of casual traders will tell you that you don't have to pay taxes on barter. Of course, there are other extremes in which people claim that bartering is illegal. (It isn't!) So is barter a permanent tax-free holiday? Don't inflate the party balloons just yet. The answer is maybe yes, maybe no. It depends on two key factors: How much are you trading, and what do you do for a living?

Our friends at the IRS (and believe us, we like to stay on the good side of those folks) don't require you to pay taxes on the value of what you barter if:

1) the barter was the "incidental sale of personal property," and

2) the trades are not part of the way you earn cash income.

The idea is that if you're trading the items in your garage, closets, shed, and so on, no tax is due. It's the other parts of the equation that can be easier to trip over. Bartering the same goods or services repeatedly can make you run afoul of the tax collector, at least in theory. If you barter goods or services that are related to the way you earn a living (your cash income), you'll owe taxes on the value of those trades. If you're a lawyer and you trade your legal eagle abilities, even if they have nothing to do with your main area of legal expertise, you will still owe income tax on those services. However, if you are a lawyer who cuts hair for friends and family on barter from time to time, you're clear of the tax man.

If you are trading at a commercial level, you will enter a whole new world of taxes, tax forms, and accounting details. At that level, Uncle Sam will require you to file a Form 1099-B in February of each year for what you purchased in the previous year. And Uncle Sam is going to tax the value of what you traded at your marginal tax rate *plus* about 15 percent self-employment tax. Your marginal tax rate will be between 15 percent and 45 percent. It's based on how much you pay in income tax on your salary and other income each year. For example, if you're like most Americans, you are taxed in the 25 percent to 45 percent tax brackets. Whichever bracket you are in is what you would pay on your barter transactions, plus the self-employment tax. So here's what it would look like on $100 in bartered goods:

$100 value in goods or services
+ **$35** (based on your income tax rate of 35 percent)
+ **$15** (based on self-employment tax rate)
= **$50** total owed to the IRS

Ouch! Weren't expecting that one, were you? To pay the correct amount of tax, you'll need to track all your transactions. If you're audited, you'll want to be able to provide that paper trail to the IRS auditor to demonstrate the full scope of your trading activity and the value of each trade.

So how is the government going to know that you traded plumbing with your neighbor Lisa, who babysat your kids? The truth is, it won't. The IRS knows about transactions only if one party reports them. (Exchange-based trades are different, and we'll get to that in a bit.) So if you don't tell Uncle Sam about installing that new shower for Lisa, and she doesn't disclose that she's been watching Billy and Abby for you each week, the government won't have a clue. That is, unless you get audited and the IRS agent wants to know about that plumbing parts supply invoice that shows you were paid cash. Mind you, we're not advocating dodging your taxes. It's just a statement of fact that unless one trader reports income from barter, there are only a few ways that the system will flag it for the IRS. However, if your barter partner reports the trade, you had better do likewise. The IRS levies hefty penalties for unreported income. Not only will you have to pay the taxes you avoided, but you'll also have to pay interest penalties that can range from 20 percent to 30 percent or more on those unpaid amounts, depending on how long you've been a scofflaw.

If you are trading with a business, you should ask the owner or manager if that trade will be reported on the company's taxes. If so, disclose for sure. Yes, it's possible that you won't get caught, but, as you've just seen, the pain is great if you do.

TAXES AND THE TRADE EXCHANGE

If you are a member of a commercial trade exchange, there's nowhere to run and nowhere to hide from the IRS. Every trade exchange must file a Form 1099-B with the IRS for all its members' trade sales for the year. Your exchange will also provide you with the same information to file with your own income taxes. Since the exchange is automatically reporting all activity to the IRS, you will have to pay taxes on the value of those trades. That's important to remember since it can considerably fatten the check you have to write to the government on April 15.

Here's an example of what can go wrong if you don't report. An art gallery employee was paid a performance bonus in artwork instead of cash. He decided to barter the art through a trade exchange and successfully sold each of the pieces he had earned. Since the exchange reported his artwork sales, and he hadn't reported it on his income taxes, the IRS came a-calling. He was found guilty of failing to report significant income on the unreported barter transactions and was told to pay thousands of dollars in taxes. So much for the bonus.

BARTER PLUS CASH

If cash is involved in any of your trades, sharpen your pencil a bit more. You need to file a Form 1099-M if the cash you received for services was over $600. Barter exchanges will report only the barter sale portion. It's up to you to report the cash received as part of your annual income for that year. Taxes will also apply on this income as well, so once again, you'll have a fatter tax bill in April.

To get the absolute lowdown on barter and taxes, check out the IRS Web site, IRS.gov, and documents like IRS

Publication 1220. For additional help, you should consult an accountant about how to handle your particular situation.

Ultimately, the tax issues boil down to your level of activity and the nature of it. Casual barter is not going to catch the eye of the IRS and is the equivalent of having a few garage sales a year. The important thing is to be aware of what you're doing and make sure you don't have to start spending all your quality time with your local IRS representative.

CHAPTER 8

CHARITY EXPANDS WITH BARTER

While we've focused on how barter can enrich your life, we realize that you may wish to help others enrich their lives, especially those who are less fortunate than you. There are an enormous number of charitable endeavors, community groups, and nonprofit organizations that help people, pets, the environment, education, and a thousand more causes. But unless you're as rich as King Midas, you probably don't have the money to support all of the good causes dear to your heart. That's where barter can come into play. By using barter as a creative method of helping your favorite cause, you expand the power of your giving beyond the limits of your wallet, credit cards, and checking account.

IN-KIND DONATIONS

Most people think that giving to charities or community groups, first and foremost, involves money. Next in most people's mind are "in-kind" donations, which are items or services rather than hard currency. In-kind donations might include donating a computer to your temple, bags of llama chow to an animal rescue group, old cell phones to shelters for abused women, or canned goods to a food bank. Both kinds of donations are essential to the survival and well-being of nonprofits.

To our minds, in-kind donations are a type of barter. While this might not be a pure tit-for-tat trade, in-kind contributions involve giving something to a cause and, in return, getting a tax deduction and the endorphin splash from doing good for someone else. Before we discuss pure barter as charitable support, please understand that we aren't suggesting you stop giving cash contributions to your favorite organizations. Those donations are essential to an organization's ability to meet its mission, which they wouldn't be able to do on barter alone.

To begin adding barter to your philanthropic work, go back and take a look at the list of stuff and skills that you compiled back in chapter 2. First, determine what you have or can do that you could give as an in-kind donation. That contribution could go directly to the group of your choice to solve a particular problem or fill a need. Some in-kind contributions will be obvious to you: donating your time to clean your house of worship, organizing an aluminum can drive for your children's school, chatting with seniors at a retirement center, and more. Karen donates her time as a motivational speaker for the nonprofit group Connections to Success, and Shera has donated her writing skills to her spiritual center's Web site and newsletter. Charitable giving helps strengthen communities, especially those that have less and need more. It also provides buckets of personal and emotional fulfillment to those doing the giving.

GIVING WITH BARTER

Barter can help you expand the impact of your charitable inclinations, because it offers some opportunities that few people consider. To get started, ask your favorite charity, group, or cause organizer for a list of needs and wants. Many organizations publish their wish lists on their Web sites or on sites like Amazon.com. Check them out to see if you can donate something directly. Then, take a look at the list to see if you have access, or know someone who does, to one or more of the items on the list. Jot down anyone you know who can put their hands on what your charity needs.

Now comes the fun part: Consider the talents, skills, services, or abilities that you have that can be traded. With those skills in mind, review the charity's list of wants to determine if there is a local company that could fill them. Contact the charity to see if the need you want to fill on its list is still current and either if it has a relationship with a vendor that supplies that good or service or if it is willing to have you contact one on its behalf. If the nonprofit gives you the green light, and better still, a contact at a vendor with which it already has a relationship, make the call. Offer to provide your service to the company in exchange for the good or service that the charity needs. Explain that the company will not only get to list the support of the charity on its Web site and in public relations communications but also receive your top-notch services at the same time. Since this is a sales job, be prepared to provide the company with a list of happy customers you have worked for, samples of your work, and any other information that would help the manager or owner recognize that you are serious about this and will provide excellent work.

Once you have an agreement in place, make sure to let the charity know which goods are coming and in what quantities. They'll be delighted, and you'll get a warm glow from doing good for a cause you believe in.

Here's how it might look: Let's say you're passionate about helping stray animals find homes. Your favorite no-kill animal shelter always needs certain items, such as dog food, towels, veterinarian services, and so on. You could offer to provide janitorial services for a local grocery store in exchange for the store donating dog food to the shelter. You (or your teenager) could volunteer to answer phones at a veterinarian's office, care for kenneled pets, clean the vet's office, or update the vet's customer database in exchange for the vet providing care for the animals at the shelter.

It might be obvious that bartering for charity, in some ways, is a lot easier for people who have a talent, skill, service, or ability that they can trade. That isn't to say that goods won't work; they will. The barter just gets more arduous. Here's how a goods barter might transpire. Let's say you make handsome gift baskets full of beautiful items. You offer a local bed-and-breakfast a certain number of gift baskets each month in exchange for donating rooms to your favorite charity. The charity could use those rooms as a prize in a "getaway" raffle, a door prize at its next fund-raiser or trivia night, or a place where out-of-town parents could stay while their sick child is in the hospital.

These sorts of barters will also work outside of a charity. If you have a friend who lacks dental insurance, you could provide your service or goods to a dentist in exchange for dental care for your friend. Charity doesn't always have to go through formal channels.

And don't overlook your employer. After all, you already know the key people there, the politics, and how to navigate within the company. Maybe your favorite charity won't be able to use a few thousand widgets from the factory where you work, but perhaps they could use the factory's van, truck, FedEx number, computer system administrator, bookkeeper, inventory control specialist, marketing director, or public relations coordinator. You can offer to trade several hours of work in exchange for the service, product, or individual your company could supply to your designated charity. (Of course, it never hurts to remind the bosses that their support of this charity will build goodwill for them in the community, especially if they publicize it.)

The power of barter is enormous if you are willing to be assertive and just *ask*.

CHARITY BEGINS AT HOME

Besides the efforts that you make on behalf of your charity, you can also encourage your favorite organization to use barter to help itself. Nonprofits can register with barter Web sites like SwapThing.com to receive bartered goods or services from members. They could also create a Meetup.com group aimed at bartering among its members and for itself. If the organization has a physical location, it can potentially use its building for barter (and cash). For instance, if your temple, church, or mosque has a commercial kitchen, it could be bartered in exchange for catered dinners for congregants, meals for the homebound or homeless, or fund-raising dinners. Classroom space can be rented or bartered, as can meeting or office space. An auditorium is a great place to barter for lectures, business meetings, and presentations or for other organizations your nonprofit supports.

We realize that some organizations, by their very nature, won't be able to open their doors to outside groups wishing to use their space. In other instances, the nonprofit or institution may not want to expose its facilities to what it perceives as potential risk. Making sure that the individual or business wanting to use the building is insured or that your group is insured against fire or other damage could remove at least one objection. If there are no fundamental reasons against putting facilities to alternative uses when they would normally be closed, you may have to build a consensus among board members or officials within the organization to explore and support using the space for others or in creative ways. For example, a woman we know who wanted to start her own catering business was able to trade catering for use of her church's commercial kitchen. The church got the dual benefit of having some of its gatherings catered, which built goodwill among the congregants, and it was also able to help a member financially support herself, her family, and her church by starting a catering business. Everybody wins!

BARTER EXCHANGES AND CHARITIES

If you are a member of a trade exchange, there are many opportunities to help a nonprofit group through barter. Many exchanges allow members to name a charity as a subaccount to their membership. You could make trades on behalf of the nonprofit for the items or services it needs. Just imagine if your place of worship needed a new roof, the elder-care center needed a new van, or the child-abuse-prevention group needed a safe house; you could help them obtain that most-needed item through the barter exchange. Even if the full price of the roof, van, or house couldn't be paid in barter credits, your organization would still save cash by deferring at least part of the cost through barter.

Members of the trade exchange could also donate credits to the charity and get a tax deduction in return. That's especially popular as the year draws to a close and brokerage members look for ways to reduce their tax bill. The exchange itself can help by putting out a call for donations on the charity's behalf as the year ends.

The nonprofit can play at an even higher level through the power of exchanged-based barter. If it joins the trade exchange, the entire world of barter opens up. Nonprofit organizations will often get reduced joining fees, lower monthly membership fees, and reduced transaction costs just for being an Internal Revenue Service 501(c)(3) nonprofit entity. Once the organization is a member of the exchange, its volunteers and members could donate goods and services to the nonprofit, which could then barter them through the exchange. The credits earned from volunteers' donations can be turned into facility repairs, furnishings, direct-mail campaigns, and a host of other goods and services. Volunteerism the barter way exponentially expands the impact of the volunteers' donated goods and labor.

Some exchanges, especially those focused primarily on individuals, allow nonprofits or community groups to join and receive a percentage of transaction fees when members name them as beneficiaries. The beauty of this system is not only that will a charitable group will get actual cash but also that individuals like you will benefit by being part of an exchange that allows you to barter for your own wants and needs. Get what you want and help your favorite cause at the same time—now *that's* leveraging the power of barter through collaboration!

BE CREATIVE

Doing good can turn into doing *great* when you add barter to your volunteer and charitable cause activities. Bartering for charity will require that you become more creative in your thinking. It may also push you to expand beyond your comfort zone by setting up barter deals on behalf of your favorite cause. But when money is limited or you just want to do more than write a check, barter can give you more options to advance the issues and causes you are passionate about. If enough supporters band together to help the cause, the impact can be profound. A beginning group can get off the ground, a struggling nonprofit can become stable, and a small group can expand the number of people, animals, or worthy needs that it helps. Barter is the hidden secret that will help make that happen.

GREAT TRADE!

Like many people around Takilma, Oregon, Stacey Williams felt like the Dome School was an important part of the community. But the prekindergarten through elementary school struggled financially despite volunteer support from parents, who not only helped keep the private school running but also donated their time to teaching and caring for the children. Stacey—who loves barter and trades Spanish lessons for gardening help—decided to resurrect the community's barter fair to benefit the Dome School. She and other parents and community members reorganized the Hope Mountain Barter Faire in 2002, turning it into a center of barter, a great weekend of entertainment and community interaction, and, most important of all, the primary fund-raiser for the school.

Each year, the fair has grown, attracting thousands of visitors and hundreds of vendors. The fair tries to be as environmentally sustainable as possible and has a zero-waste policy. It operates a community kitchen for attendees to prepare their own meals using plates, pans, and utensils that they wash for reuse as the fair goes on. Hundreds of volunteers earn their $10 admission to the fair by helping to set it up, run it, and take it down each fall. During the event, there are "freecycle" tables of stuff that community residents have donated. Fairgoers, especially kids, can fill a basket with freecycle items they can then use to trade with vendors.

The vendors are encouraged to barter as well as accept cash. In the process, children and people new to the barter-fair concept learn the value of trading. It helps those with limited means, seniors on fixed incomes, and others who are struggling financially to get what they want and need without having to spend a dime. The fair also lifts residents' spirits as the dreary autumn and winter months approach by providing entertainment from musicians, artisans, and dancers. There are also plenty of local farmers who barter their produce to lighten the pressure on residents' wallets.

Best of all, as a tremendous fund-raiser for the Dome School, the fair helps replace several annual fund-raisers that were producing little revenue and required a lot of work. Between admission fees, sales of T-shirts, and vendor booth fees, the fair raises $12,000 to $13,000 a year for the school. That money goes a long way toward renovating the building, keeping it up-to-date with disabled-accessible bathrooms, and adding books and other classroom supplies that would have been difficult to afford or were even unobtainable before.

Stacey notes that the fair not only supports the school but it also strengthens the community by gathering everyone together for a good cause and to practice a lot of great trades.

GREAT TRADE!

As a single mother of four kids, Tammy Bunn knew what it's like to struggle to keep a family fed, housed, and healthy. So when she remarried and gained a bit of breathing room, she decided that she wanted to do something to help other mothers, as well as her own family. She started the Barter4Kids children's clothing exchange in

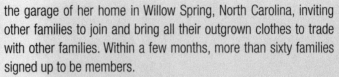

the garage of her home in Willow Spring, North Carolina, inviting other families to join and bring all their outgrown clothes to trade with other families. Within a few months, more than sixty families signed up to be members.

Families contribute clothes that they tag and price according to whatever value they believe they are worth. (Sometimes Tammy tells them to increase the price if they have marked an item too low.) Whatever the total dollar value of the clothing adds up to, that's how much credit the family has on account to spend. Then, on several Saturdays a year, Tammy opens the doors to her garage, and the families get to spend their credits on "new" clothes. The barter sale has become so popular that she opens by appointment on occasion as well. She charges $8 cash each time a family shops by appointment and $15 for a regularly scheduled sale.

But Tammy doesn't stop there. Families will also bring in toys, baby equipment, unused baby food, and more. Two area churches call her when they have missionaries or families in need. Maybe it's a family who has returned from a tropical mission posting and has no winter clothes for its children. Tammy gathers up items from her stock and donates them to the churches. Before school started one year, Tammy took two backpacks that had been brought in for barter and filled them with school supplies. She took the proceeds from membership fees, as well as the $15 fee she charges each family to shop during the Saturday sales, and bought four more backpacks. She filled those with supplies as well and donated them to families who had no money to outfit their kids for the school year.

For all the times people helped her when she was a single mom, struggling to care for her family, Tammy says barter is her way of giving back and making life a little easier for someone else. It's also a way to help people she has never met who are in need, none of which would happen in quite the same way if cash was the only currency in the world.

TRADING TIP

Look for homegrown barter exchanges that admit individuals as well as organizations. Invite your community group, charity, or religious institution to become part of the exchange and have its members and volunteers trade on its behalf.

TRADING TIP

Start a barter volunteer group for your favorite nonprofit organization and work together to find ways to trade that will help the organization. Ask the members to fill out a skills, talent, knowledge, and stuff survey to discover what they have that could be bartered. In some cases, those skills or goods can be donated directly to the organization. In others, they could be traded on an exchange, in a barter club the group starts, or among the organization's supporters for the benefit of the nonprofit. Start small, gather a group of committed volunteers, and then expand as everyone gets the hang of barter and becomes more adventurous in their trading exploits.

CHAPTER 9

CHILD'S PLAY: BARTER FOR KIDS

Barter is such a simple skill that it shouldn't be left only to adults. Why should they have all the fun? Let's get the kids in on the action. Children naturally want to barter all the time. In the lunchroom, one kid will trade her Oreos for another's Twinkies. Boys have traded baseball cards, marbles, and comic books for ages. Teenage girls will swap dresses, jeans, jewelry, and other articles of clothing to broaden their wardrobe and get a quick new look for free. Smaller kids will swap toys for a week or two, just . . . because.

When children trade, they develop a sense that they have power to earn their way in the world beyond what Mom and Dad give them for allowance or what they are paid at their after-school job. Barter broadens their perception of how to navigate the world of personal and professional commerce. It also teaches them how to negotiate, play fair, value a good or service, make new friends, determine what they really want, delay gratification, and forge relationships so that everyone wins. It can even teach them the basics of entrepreneurship and how to start a small business.

RULES OF ENGAGEMENT

Since children are natural traders, there are some excellent strategies you can employ to encourage their barter habits so they will carry those great skills into adulthood. Instead of having them jump in unfettered, you need to establish some ground rules.

First and foremost, teach children that barter is about the fair exchange of goods and services. Direct trades are often unbalanced, but when that happens between willing adults, no one can complain. After all, each participant understood the rules of the game going in and negotiated for the best deal possible. But if an older kid takes advantage of a younger child's naïveté by getting more than he or she gives, that teaches sneakiness, reinforces greed, and will eventually engender hard feelings in the younger child and his or her parents. The simplest way to teach fair trade is to invoke the Golden Rule, even if you aren't the religious sort. When you treat people the way you want to be treated, no one gets hurt, and everyone wins. Simple. Direct. Fair. Barter, even more so than in the cash world, relies on honor and fair dealing because relationships are formed in the act of trading. Besides, who wants to keep trading with someone who is an opportunist or a cheater?

Supervise your child's first trades to make sure he or she has got the hang of it. That's especially important if they've never seen you trade before and if they are under the age of twelve, when barter with rules will be completely new (and, we hope, exciting) to them. Ideally, young children will trade within the family first. Then they can branch out with friends at school, with neighbors, and then with others they already know. Teenagers can try out trading with strangers via Web sites like CraigsList, bulletin boards, or even flea markets. But it's wise for a parent to track trades with strangers because, let's face it, the world can be a dangerous place. If your offspring are posting trade ads on the Internet, bulletin boards, or other public venues, make sure they don't list your physical address—just a cell phone or an e-mail address that can be monitored by an adult. Also, check the rules of Web sites they want to trade on. Most barter sites don't allow trading for anyone under the age of eighteen.

Set clear guidelines on what your kids can trade. If Emily detests going to ballet lessons and trades away her ballet shoes and leotards for a monster bag of candy, you're not going to be overjoyed if you intended for her to keep up with her pliés. One helpful rule of thumb is to allow kids to trade what they have purchased with their own money and for their own use. For anything else, they have to ask Mom or Dad first. That means they can't trade away the puce sweater from Aunt Erma, their brother's turtle, the cookies Mom just baked, or Dad's golf clubs, unless you give them the green light.

Before older kids begin trading, or if they have an offer from someone else, they should have an idea of the value of that item other than "Hey Mom, I *really, really* want this." Encourage them to do a quick check of Web sites such as eBay and CraigsList or retailers like Kmart or Amazon.com to find out what other people are asking for similar items. They need to take into account the condition of the item or their ability to perform the work before they trade. Ask them to figure out what a new item in mint condition is worth. Then try to calculate what their item (or their partner's offering) is worth, considering its condition.

If they are trading Rollerblades that are scuffed, dirty, and heavily used—in other words, fair condition—what are the skates worth compared with brand-new skates? This is an excellent opportunity for them to learn about real-life economics. It's the type of lesson that will stay with them forever and will carry over in later life, such as when they are haggling for a car or a home. They will also learn to be more careful consumers. Instead of just grabbing an item without asking questions, they'll learn to examine it more carefully, look for any flaws or issues that could affect its use, and see if it's really worth the asking price. We don't want to teach kids to be jaded, especially at a young age, but we do want them to be savvy consumers and good, but fair, negotiators.

Before your child seals a deal, make sure you have final approval. The same should apply if the deal is with another child. That child's parent or guardian should be able to say yea or nay to the trade so you don't wind up with unhappy parents whose child traded away the brand-new math flash cards they just bought. If your child is trading with an adult whom you know and trust, then there's less need to oversee the transaction. Either way, let your son or daughter know that if you don't approve of the deal, it can't transpire, or, if it already has, the trade will have to be undone.

Encourage your kids to track their trades in a journal or on the computer so they can see how successful they have been. Tracking can be a big self-esteem builder. We have a tendency not to acknowledge our accomplishments. Often those around us fail to recognize them as well. But as your children barter again and again, negotiating one successful trade after another, they will realize that they can negotiate and make deals happen. They will begin to appreciate their capacity to make a deal. If they record the estimated dollar value of each trade, they will see the increasing power of their ability to provide for themselves or at least to acquire extras that they want. They can develop a sense of pride at their growing list of transactions.

This is especially true if they are trading their labor or knowledge (rather than stuff). When children trade the work of their hands (such as yard care), their skills (such as playing guitar), or knowledge (such as surfing lessons), they discover that they have worth far beyond just what they own. They begin to equate power in their world with what they can do and how creative they can be, and they will learn that there are more ways to obtain what they want and need than simply by using the almighty dollar.

They will also develop a sense of sharing and community, especially among their friends and family members. Encourage them to share tasks—in particular, the ones they don't care for—with their friends or siblings in exchange for helping with the friends' or siblings' chores. For example, if your son is expected to rake the deluge of fall leaves from the yard, and he is less than enthusiastic, suggest that he get help from a buddy to do the job in exchange for raking the buddy's yard as well. In other cases, the kids can trade jobs they dislike for a less-distasteful job that their brother or sister would be happy to exchange. If you allow children latitude with the chores they trade, you'll probably get a more-cooperative youngster and participating family member.

To cut down on the amount of whining for new toys, one parent suggests joining a local individual exchange. When the kids start complaining that they're bored with their existing toys and demand new ones, tell the little guys that they can list any of their old toys for trade with the exchange. They can then trade these toys for ones they do want, or, depending on the organization of the exchange, they can use the credit from the trade to barter for other toys. While this method may not cut down completely on the whining and boredom, it will at least begin teaching children how to barter and give them an option for obtaining what they want without pestering you for cash or a bigger allowance.

As they start to grasp what bartering is all about, they can teach their younger siblings and other kids in the neighborhood how to trade. Spreading the word about barter not only helps them to create more potential trading partners but also strengthens their network of friends and neighbors, building a better community. At the same time, it empowers those they teach, just as they were empowered. Your children could offer to teach bartering at meetings of Girl and Boy Scouts (maybe even earning a badge in American business, labor, or culture), youth groups, community groups, after-school programs, Future Farmers of America, Junior Achievement, and other such groups.

Older kids have an opportunity to turn learning into barter opportunities and, potentially, into a future expertise or even a profession. If your son or daughter is curious about a particular skill, an apprenticeship with an expert in that field is the beginning of learning that skill and mastering it later on. That sort of skill or capability can turn into a barter-able ability that will produce great rewards for your kids. For example, if your child is interested in cutting hair, throwing a ceramic pot, repairing engines, or making guitars, she could apprentice herself to someone who knows that job well. By trading her time, labor, and willingness to learn, she could slowly become a hairstylist, ceramist, mechanic, or luthier. Once she has mastered the skills, she can then ply her new "trade" for cash and barter. Simply by bartering her time, your child has opened a door to an exciting new pastime and maybe even a source of income for years to come.

Bartering can even become a pathway to college. Some colleges and universities accept barter in exchange for tuition. Some, like La Roche College in Pittsburgh, Pennsylvania, are members of barter brokerages and accept trade credits for tuition. Others, such as Lindenwood University in St. Charles, Missouri, accept direct trades for tuition. Imagine your high school senior helping to raise livestock or trading her Web site development skills to earn tuition to college.

Once your children have mastered the basics of bartering, they can turn it into other forms of academic gold. They can write school reports, essays, and extra credit term papers on it for language arts, economics, sociology, civics, and history classes. (Did you know that 400 communities issued their own barter currency during the Great Depression?) You can bet that barter will be a subject their teachers won't have read about a few gazillion times before, and your students will simultaneously score some extra credit and brownie points for writing about such an unusual subject. (For teachers who want to incorporate barter into their classroom lessons, see the sample lesson plan in the Resources section.)

WHERE TO TRADE?

Many places are available for kids to barter, although some will require adult supervision or permission. The most logical and first spot should be bartering in the home. Trading with siblings is a great way to get started, and you can help the beginners with logistics. Family is the best place to start since any mistakes or misunderstandings will be easy to correct and put right. After that, the easiest spots will be with your extended family members (aunts, uncles, cousins, grand-parents, etc.), neighborhood, place of worship, community center, school, social groups, and the like.

In the online world, there are also great Web sites such as U-Exchange that offer bartering. Many require that partici-pants be eighteen years old or older, so parents will have to be involved. As we mentioned before, we encourage you to limit trades for newbies, younger children, or those involving people you don't know so that only older teens trade on the Internet with adult supervision, and no child, no matter the age, is trading with a stranger.

The online world also offers some other trading possibilities for your kids that are less direct. They could post a few of their wants and their haves on their Facebook page or send out tweets with the same mini lists. Your kids might even be able to persuade their school's parent-teacher organization to let them send out barter announcements to their e-mail list or on their Google, Yahoo! or other invitation-only online group.

The various barter groups to be found on Meetup.com offer a different take on Web site trading. This community and social networking site gives individuals the possibility to set up their own barter clubs via the Internet. Groups invite members and can exchange e-mail and notices aimed at organizing face-to-face meetings that allow the group members to trade. Check to see if there is a Meetup.com barter group in your town. (If there isn't and you're feeling spunky, you could start one!) Some sites are dedicated to specific types of bartering, such as homegrown food, alternative healing providers, small business, moms, collecting, and lots more. Be aware that some groups will charge a membership fee, often nominal, to join.

If a neighbor is having a garage sale, and your little one spots something he or she wants at the sale, that's a perfect time for him or her to offer a trade. Maybe she could trade for whatever she wants by folding clothes during the event or helping to clean up afterward; perhaps your son could carry items to buyers' cars or cart trash to the bin or turn unsold goods into new barter items. Whatever your son or daughter is willing and capable of doing, he or she can begin the conversation with the garage sale holder and see what sort of help is needed.

If you have joined a barter exchange, your children could come aboard as subaccounts. You'll need to add them yourself and make sure they understand that barter-exchange trades have cash costs and must be approved by Mom and Dad. Because there is such a wide array of goods available on exchanges, you will definitely have to be involved in this sort of trading. It will also require educating your children about what the limits are to their bartering. Think of children and brokerages as giving your children a credit card. Imagine that the membership is like sending your kids to the mall with a credit card that has no limit. Would you want to just set them free and say, "Have fun"? Set a limit on how much they can barter each month. You may even want to liken it to an allowance or call it just that so they understand there are finite amounts involved and using the exchange is a privilege, not a right.

Many towns have flea markets, swap meets, farmers' markets, or barter fairs (or *faires,* as it is often spelled) that offer a cornucopia of trading opportunities. Kids can take their items with them to the event and see if vendors will trade with them. Since these gatherings aren't limited to charging a fixed price, and haggling is a way of life, barter is not just accepted, it's encouraged. At barter fairs, kids and adults alike are encouraged to volunteer their labor to set up, operate, and take down the fair to keep costs low for the often-volunteer operators. Older kids who have become experienced traders may want to set up their own booth to trade goods. Some fairs even have a "freecycle" table where kids can drop off items and pick up others that they can travel around the fair with, offering to swap for vendors' items. It's truly an event that is intended to empower people of all ages to get into the barter habit.

Other trading partners can be found among neighbors, school friends, fellow members at places of worship, bulletin boards at grocery stores, your children's own Web site if they're tech savvy, and a swap meet they organize in your driveway or at school. (Don't wait for others to organize it; help them do it!)

To a lesser degree, trading with established retailers or businesses is possible as well. Kids will likely have more luck with a locally owned company rather than a larger chain, following basically the same rules that apply to adults who want to trade. Young people just need to take a look at what their interests and abilities are and what the needs of the business might be before making an offer. Perhaps the local pizza parlor that holds kids' birthday parties would like a party wrangler to help out on Saturdays in exchange for free sodas and pizza for the wrangler? Maybe one of your town's car dealers could use a car detailer on weekends in exchange for working toward owning a used car? Does the corner barbershop need someone to sweep up hair and answer phones? Keep in mind that they'll have to abide by child labor law restrictions. Ultimately, anything is possible for a child or teenager who is motivated and supported in the great adventure that is bartering.

GREAT TRADE!

Cedar Braaten learned how to barter by the time he was barely out of diapers. Of course, it helped that his mom, Stacey Williams, is a big barter fan as well. It was only natural that she taught her son what she knew. As an eleven-year-old rock hound, he loves trading with others for crystals and stones he doesn't have. He is also pretty savvy when it comes to bartering for used bikes, fixing them up, and then selling them for cash. After all, an eleven-year-old's allowance when there are three other siblings in the house goes only so far.

Probably his best trade was exchanging a bracelet he got for free for a fishing downrigger. (Downriggers cost at least $100 new and often cost five to eight times more than that.) That was especially sweet because Cedar didn't have a downrigger, and he really wanted one. If he'd had to rely on the typical eleven-year-old's allowance alone, he might have been shaving before he could have afforded to buy one.

Cedar trades with his thirteen-year-old sister, Sadie, but he's learned that trading with his younger brothers, seven-year-old Jaden and four-year-old Tabor, can be frustrating. They barter, but later, they take back what they traded. Cedar says he'll trade with them when they're older. Maybe.

TRADING TIPS FOR KIDS

- Don't start trading without your parents' approval.
- Start with family and friends.
- Make a list of what you can offer to trade.
- Make another list of what you want.
- Get an idea of what your items are worth.
- Get an idea of what someone else's goods/services are worth.
- Ask your neighbors if you can trade with them.
- Trade with strangers only with your parents' permission.
- Trade fair! Treat people the way you want to be treated.
- Ask your mom or dad to take you to a barter fair. Tell them they might make some great trades themselves, and they'll definitely have fun.

LET'S MAKE A LIST

Here are some lists you can copy to keep track of what you have available to trade, who you've traded with, and how much you've saved or earned in barter. To get started, ask yourself these three questions:

1) What do I *have* to barter with? (Examples: sweaters, shoes, or sporting goods you have outgrown)
2) What can I *do* that I could barter? (Examples: cleaning, babysitting, or bike repair)
3) What do I *know* that I could barter? (Examples: teaching someone math, how to knit, how to ski, or how to play guitar)

Have fun bartering!

WHAT I HAVE TO TRADE

Item/Service	Estimated Value

What Can You Trade?

Here's a list of some barter possibilities for kids:

Accessories
Babysitting
Baking
Baseball cards
Bikes
Birthday party "wrangler" (assistant)
Board games
Books
Bulb planting
Car detailing
Car repair
Car washing
Caring for livestock
Cat grooming
CDs
Chauffeuring
Clean out people's garages, attics, sheds
Clothes
Collectibles
Companion for the elderly
Computer and video games
Cooking
Creating Web sites
Data entry
Dating coach
Dog grooming
Dog training
Dog walking
DVDs
Fashion consultant
Hairstyling (braiding, coloring, cutting)
Hedge trimming
Hitting coach
Hold yard sales for people
House painting
Housecleaning
House-sitting
Internet research
Jewelry
Knitting
Lawn mower repairs
Lawn mowing
Leaf raking
Makeup application
Making greeting cards
Oil changes or other car repairs
Old and/or unused musical instruments
Old and/or unused sports equipment
Painting old or found furniture
Paintings
Pet sitting
Planting gardens
Poop scooping
Refinishing old or found furniture
Rides to school
Room decorating
Scooters

Sewing
Snow shoveling
Teach a language
Teach guitar or other musical
    instruments
Teach skateboarding
Teach skiing, baseball, or other
    sports
Term-paper proofreading

Toys
Tutoring
Unused game consoles
Use of your skateboard, baseball,
    or other sports equipment
Watering gardens
Weeding gardens
Window washing

CHAPTER 10

BARTER AND YOUR NEW SMALL BUSINESS

If you embrace the barter lifestyle, you may find that it becomes a bigger and bigger part of enriching your personal life. You will figure out what you have to barter, and if you get exceptionally good at it, you may even have a little cottage industry built around barter and a trade exchange. But what about your life on the job? How does barter fit into your work life?

At first it may not seem like barter at work would be much of an option. We've said all along that cash is king, and if you can get cash for your labor or stuff, take it. That certainly applies to the place where you earn a paycheck. But you may be one of the 50 percent of Americans who loathes their job. In many of those cases, a new job isn't going to make those employees jump out of bed every morning, delighted at the prospect of going to work that day.

Many people have a yearning, a hope, a dream, or maybe a deeply buried desire to start their own business. In fact, about two-thirds of Americans say they'd like to start their own company. But money is almost always the major obstacle that stops them. Many people's small-business desires die before they even have a chance to be planted because these budding entrepreneurs couldn't envision a way to get the money necessary to get started. Either they need the financial resources to feed and shelter their families or they need health care and therefore can't quit their job. In other instances, they must have large amounts of capital to buy a building and the equipment to get started. And in most cases, it's all three. In the face of such a major obstacle, many people give up and just stay stuck in their miserable jobs.

But it doesn't have to be that way. If money is all that is separating you from your dream of starting your own small business—ta-da! Barter to the rescue. Barter can help ease the tremendous costs of launching a business. Barter can give you an avenue to get started, even if you have only minimal cash, and it can apply to every single aspect of start-up costs. Barter can help you maximize the cash you have and leverage the power of your products or services to acquire what you need to get going and grow. We have seen barter push a small business from the brink of disaster to profitability, all by establishing a few key trading relationships. It can take you from hopeless to hopeful in just a few easy steps.

LEVERAGING THE POWER OF BARTER

We're quite serious when we say that barter can apply to every aspect of your business before you even open the doors (or launch the Web site or set up the home office). If you've already got a cottage business in motion, keep rolling—but take the time to write a business plan if you haven't done so already. Even if you haven't started your company yet, a business plan is essential to keeping you focused on what your business is and how you are going to make it successful. A business plan doesn't have to be elaborate, but it should cover the basics, including

- who your competition is and how much they charge for their product or service,
- who your prospective customers are,
- your marketing plan,
- how you plan to operate the business,
- who your key employees will be, and
- your financial projections (these will tell you what you need to operate monthly and when you'll start making a profit, if you aren't already).

There's one last important point regarding your business plan: Barter should be an integral part of it.

WHY BARTER?

Obviously, you recognize that you have tremendous potential to save money on your start-up by bartering for what you need, but there are some other excellent reasons to barter that you probably haven't even considered. In fact, many business owners miss out on opportunities to barter; it's like they're in the midst of battle with a secret weapon in their armory that they refuse to use.

By bartering, you will automatically generate your first customers. But they won't be just any run-of-the-mill customers. Because it takes more interaction to buy and sell through barter, you'll get to know these business owners beyond the mere transaction level. The relationships you create with your barter partners will build the basis for your first satisfied customers, who will serve as one of the most potent forces in promoting your new business: word-of-mouth advertising. These won't be people who just walk in off the street or click over from a browser. These are your business allies who will get to know you and your business plan; in most cases, they will want to help you succeed, just as they wanted to succeed when they got started. If you treat them well, they will become your cheerleaders.

When your barter partners vouch for your business to their customers and vendors, you begin to build your brand to future customers you may not have been able to attract otherwise, even with a hefty advertising budget. Just think: If you started your business on a shoestring, you might have only two or three customers in your first few weeks of operation. But with your barter customers, you'll have clients before you even officially open the doors. These clients will be able to offer testimonials to their customers and within your community. They can also post testimonials on your Web site, your blog, your Facebook page, and your Twitter account. Of course, you'll want to offer your customers your own testimonials in return, along with your company name, to post on their Internet and social networking sites. Providing testimonials for your trading partners builds even more goodwill with them while simultaneously spreading your company name. Sneaky and savvy, all at the same time.

By associating yourself with established companies that have sterling reputations, your start-up will also get a boost. When you can list a respected firm as one of your strategic partners, your company automatically earns more respect and credibility in the marketplace. You go from being a fledging upstart to an innovative business with esteemed partners who inherently boost your profile and the appearance of stability among competitors.

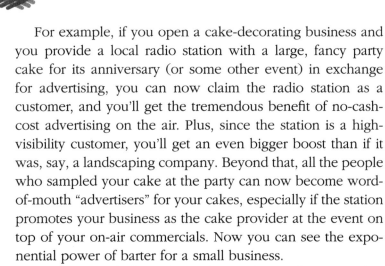

For example, if you open a cake-decorating business and you provide a local radio station with a large, fancy party cake for its anniversary (or some other event) in exchange for advertising, you can now claim the radio station as a customer, and you'll get the tremendous benefit of no-cash-cost advertising on the air. Plus, since the station is a high-visibility customer, you'll get an even bigger boost than if it was, say, a landscaping company. Beyond that, all the people who sampled your cake at the party can now become word-of-mouth "advertisers" for your cakes, especially if the station promotes your business as the cake provider at the event on top of your on-air commercials. Now you can see the exponential power of barter for a small business.

Besides word-of-mouth marketing, barter draws in other customers that you might not have attracted without having to spend large amounts of cash on promotions such as advertising and e-mail or direct-mail campaigns. When you provide gift certificates for your products or services to your barter partners in trade for their items, you create the opportunity to attract more new customers. Your trading partner is going to hand those gift certificates out in a variety of ways, but they will all go into the hands of people you most likely haven't met yet and who don't know about your business. If satisfied, they will bring their cash business to you and then refer you to even more of their friends and colleagues.

As new customers begin showing up, you will create a growing momentum around your business. That positive energy can be felt by customers, vendors, colleagues, and maybe even the banker, who will give you a much-appreciated cash infusion when you need it. Don't make the mistake of thinking momentum is a soft, airy-fairy notion that lacks substance. Momentum translates into real money. Think of the difference between going into a store where there are plenty of customers shopping, chatting, and buying versus going into a store where there's no one stirring except you and the owner, who looks a little desperate for sales. Or how about those times you've dined at a new restaurant when there were maybe one or two couples at other tables and the servers were tripping over themselves with nothing to do versus going into a bustling eatery full of smiling, talking patrons, happily sampling new dishes and taking in the atmosphere? When you compare those scenarios, the difference boils down to the momentum, buzz, and interest the business is generating. That momentum converts into hard cash.

Bartering as a novice entrepreneur teaches you valuable business negotiation skills that will carry over into cash-based purchasing. While many barter deals are straightforward, some will involve a bit of negotiation—a good skill to have. Even if you attended business school, these sorts of "street smarts" are invaluable in helping your company to grow.

Barter can help relieve some of the worry, fear, and emotional upheaval of starting a business. When cash is tight, our fears tend to pull our nerves taut. By creating barter relationships that guarantee you will attract customers, you will worry less about where the money will come from to get started and continue operations. Less stress means you are more pleasant to your employees, spouse, partner, children, and even clients. A frazzled owner definitely has an impact on the operation of the business, and it's rarely positive.

Lower stress also means you're more creative in your thinking. If the ceaseless hamsters of worry aren't racing around your mental wheel, you'll have more energy to put into thinking through how to solve problems, how to market to new customers, how to deal effectively with crises when they arise, and maybe even how to develop the next phase of your product or service. Being a creative thinker and problem solver is an essential ingredient for any entrepreneur, and barter relieves you of some of the worry that withers that creative muscle.

Barter for business also frees up your time to do the work you love and not to have to do as much of the activities you dislike or aren't adept at. For instance, you could clean the bathrooms, scrub the break room, landscape the grounds, water the interior plants, launder the mats, and do a whole host of other maintenance duties. Or you could barter with janitorial, landscaping, and mat-cleaning services to do all that work for you. You could then spend your time selling more, creating more, and generally working on your business. Isn't your time better spent working on your company rather than washing windows?

Because barter enables you to save cash for other purposes, you can smooth out some of the roller-coaster ride of slow sales versus heavy-volume cycles. Whether it's feast and the greenbacks are flowing or famine and they aren't, you'll have a source of cash that you would otherwise have had to commit to essential operations. When cash-flow dips even out, you worry less about survival. You are able to purchase your raw materials or pay employees so that you have plenty of products on hand and the people to sell them. Barter gives you cash-flow peace of mind.

GETTING EXPERT HELP

No serious business that we know of is able to function without an accountant, bookkeeper, or lawyer at one time or another. The nature of small businesses often requires the use of these professionals and many others to help you get started and grow like gangbusters. The more complex the business you are starting, the higher the likelihood that you will need professional assistance in some form. Maybe you need a prototype firm to help create a working model of your idea or invention. Perhaps you need a lawyer to help you incorporate your company and an accountant to advise you on tax issues. You might even need a Web site developer, a graphic artist to design your logo, a database specialist to create your customer contact system, or a computer tech to set up your network. All of these professionals can be essential to small-business success, and they can put a big dent in your wallet when you use them. Barter can help divert your cash from the expense of these experts into other areas where you need it.

Besides getting essential services, barter can also help you contract with professionals or consultants that you wouldn't be able to afford if cash was your only option. Let's say you need a programmer to develop software for your company, and you don't have anywhere near enough money to afford that service. You can barter your company's product or service for the software developer's work without burning through all your cash. In the same way, you might have enough money to afford a general attorney, but maybe what you really need is a more sophisticated law firm that can help you obtain a patent or protect an invention or intellectual property—services that a general attorney isn't experienced with. Chances are good that you won't be able to afford the hundreds of dollars an hour that big-firm lawyers charge, but if you use barter, you can get access to those legal eagles and protect yourself fully under the law.

KEEPING EMPLOYEES HAPPY

When you first open a business, finding the right employees can have an impact on your company's success. You'll put a lot of effort into finding good workers and paying money for help-wanted ads, and then, once workers are hired, you'll spend hours of your time training them. That effort and time has a real value even if you were the one doing the searching and providing the training. You could have spent that time on sales or doing something else that produced money for your company, so there truly is a cost to searching for and training employees.

To make the most of your time and effort, you want to keep your valued employees on the job. If they quit, you've lost all the time and deferred earnings you invested in them. Plus, you'll have to start the hunt all over again for a replacement. When you're just getting started, chances are you won't be able to pay your staff top dollar, so you need to find a way to reward them for being loyal, hardworking employees. Barter can help you do that. You can pay your employees part of their salary in barter or add to their compensation with barter scrip or gift certificates to restaurants, dentists, or other businesses that they would appreciate. You save on payroll expenses and keep your employees happy at the same time.

Barter can also help you set up a system of employee rewards for whatever goals you want them to meet. Maybe it's being the employee of the month, making a certain number of sales each week, or making a targeted number of cold calls every month. Karen would regularly reward her employees with performance bonuses such as tickets to the circus that they could use for their families. Shera and her coworkers received a giant cookie on their birthdays as a gift from their employer, who was a member of a trade exchange. Prizes such as trips or restaurant certificates are easily obtained through barter for those incentive programs. You can allow your employees a certain amount in bartered goods and services from your own business, or, if you are a member of an exchange, you'll have a wide range of items to choose from. You can let your employees choose barter scrip or gift certificates from restaurants, spas, grocery stores, shops, boutiques, or any other business that they would appreciate.

You can also reward employees for excellent sales, extra effort, employment anniversaries, birthdays, or any other reason with scrip or gift certificates. Once employees understand how to use scrip (if that's the form of the reward you choose), they will be delighted at the gift or incentive, and you'll have a happier employee who will want to work harder and stay with you longer.

Employees aren't the only ones you can reward with trade credits or gift certificates obtained through barter. Give your best customers certificates from your barter partners. They won't know you bartered for them, and they will feel valued and honored that you rewarded their loyalty and patronage. Building that sort of goodwill means they will want to return to do more and more business with you.

If you have vendors or colleagues who refer customers to you, you can reward them with bartered gifts as well. You can bet that when it comes time to refer someone again, they'll choose you rather than your competitors—all because you built up such goodwill by giving them a great gift certificate to a restaurant or for a game of golf. Those sorts of relationships will carry your business a long way toward stability and growth.

WHEN CASH AND BARTER BLEND

In some barter deals, cash is a part of the transaction. This tends to be more the case in direct barter than exchange-based barter. As a buyer, if you are doing a cash–barter blend, you can decide if it's right for you by finding the fair market price for the item and making sure you are paying an equitable amount of combined cash and barter. Even if the cash portion is half of the price, keep in mind that you will still be getting the item for less cash than you would have paid without the barter component.

There are times when you will want to be the partner who requires cash as part of a trade. For many start-ups, money is so tight that they may have to charge a portion of the sale in cash. For example, if your business is construction, you should require cash up front for the cost of lumber, concrete, or other raw materials that will be out-of-pocket expenses. But for a service business, knowing when to require cash is easier. Basically, if you have hard costs that must come out of your business revenue, you can charge cash for those expenses. In fact, some barter-exchange members make it a practice to charge a cash blend for things like construction, new vehicles, and large printing jobs. If you have low cash flow, that's an excellent time to sell for cash and barter. You could charge cash for the fixed cost of producing your goods and barter for the remainder of the purchase price. Over time, you may find that you can convert pure barter customers into cash customers if you have established a good relationship with them and they truly desire your goods or service. But you'll have to request that they switch to cash only or specify that you will accept cash only from that point forward—a risky move because they might decide to take their business elsewhere.

GETTING A LOAN ON BARTER

Since most entrepreneurs struggle because they have so little cash to work with, there is another lender most aren't aware of. Barter exchanges will often extend a credit line to their members, even new ones. In other instances members can take out a loan through their exchange. New exchange members often start with a credit line when they join so they have some latitude to begin trading. The amount of credit an exchange issues is typically based on how much demand there is for your product or service, whether you're in good standing with the exchange, and the business or individual's credit report. If you're a hypnotist and there's not a huge clamor for hypnosis in the exchange, you probably will get only a small credit line. If your business is a fine dining restaurant, you're more likely to a get a substantial line.

If your credit is poor or less than sterling, you may not get a line of credit from the exchange or get only a small one to start out. Once you've proven yourself, you'll be able to access more credit. How well you treat people can also affect the amount you get. If your fellow exchange members report that doing business with you is easy and they are getting good value from the transaction, you'll likely get a higher line of credit than if members find that you're resistant to trades, that you inflate the price of your products, or that you provide poor customer service. Exchanges are a business like any other, and they want to keep their customers happy just like you do (or should want to, of course). If you reach your credit line, your account will be frozen from more purchases unless you can negotiate a higher credit limit with your broker. That won't be difficult if you have a solid track record with your exchange.

Loans, on the other hand, are typically for a set amount of trade credits and will also have an interest rate attached. While most exchanges don't charge interest on a line of credit, some do, so it's important to ask before you commit yourself. One big advantage of applying for a loan through an exchange is that there is usually less paperwork; also, you typically won't have to provide financial records or have to undergo a credit check if you're an established exchange member. If you're new to the exchange, a credit report is much more likely.

At times you will have to put up collateral, depending on how large the loan amount is. The loan and interest will be repaid with barter credits that you earn by doing business with other exchange members. Look at your annual trading volume to determine how large of a loan you might be able to qualify for. If you haven't been a member of an exchange for that long, or you've been in business for only a short while, evaluate how likely the exchange membership will be to use your business and how much trade credit you might be able to generate each year. Make your proposal to your broker, and remember that you may be able to negotiate your terms and rates, especially if the brokerage is locally owned. To argue the case for a larger loan, you could offer to pitch members your product or service, and the exchange owner can base the amount of your loan or credit line on the future business his or her members have committed to. You'll have a monthly repayment schedule, but you will still be able to trade beyond that amount.

If you aren't ready for a trade exchange, you can still use barter to get start-up capital. Propose to a business owner you know (or have a connection to) that he or she give you a loan with interest that you will repay with services/ products from your company. This approach works especially well with companies that can use your goods and services repeatedly. When Karen started her two magazines, she approached a couple of business owners she knew and asked for cash loans of $2,500 from each of them. One of the owners accepted payment solely in the form of advertising in her magazines. He received double the value of the loan in advertising to repay the loan and interest. The other business owner received a combination of ads and cash in repayment. For Karen, these cash infusions came at an absolutely critical moment of survival for her young company, and without them, the magazines would have folded.

Karen also used barter scrip to pay her magazine's writers, photographers, and graphic designers. Her staff were able to receive part of their pay in trade credits at the exchange where she was a member. They used them for gift certificates to restaurants and other retailers. Those deals lowered her personnel costs while allowing her to use valuable freelancers to produce the magazines and fill their pages with stories and photos. Karen took it a step further and bartered for answering, accounting, and legal services. In all, she saved about 70 percent of her cash start-up costs by trading. She also opened the business more quickly because she could use her cash for other needs that were not available through barter. At the same time, she attracted more cash customers because others saw businesses already advertising in her magazines. Barter not only was the fast track to getting started for Karen but was also the lifeline that kept her in business once it was up and running.

Barter can certainly do the same for you if you get that entrepreneurial urge.

GREAT TRADE!

When Michelle Nelson decided to start Back 2 Basics Marketing, she had just moved to St. Louis, knew only one person, had no business contacts, and had only a few hundred dollars to support herself and her son. Michelle immediately signed up with two local barter exchanges before she officially opened her doors. Within weeks, she had attracted several clients thanks to being promoted by the exchanges. Along with $5,000 in a new-member credit line from the exchanges, she earned barter credits from clients that allowed her to outfit her office with desks, chairs, filing cabinets, and the like, as well as print business cards and magnetic signs for her car. Shortly after she began delivering for her clients, Michelle got a delightful surprise. Her clients referred her to their colleagues and vendors, who then became cash customers. And the cash-paying referrals just kept coming.

Within two years, Back 2 Basics Marketing had six employees and multiple interns and was doing a booming business, all thanks to Michelle's hard work—and the power of barter, of course.

TRADING TIP

When you're trying to figure out how much barter you should do, use this rule of thumb: Set a goal of 3 percent to 10 percent of your total sales (known as gross revenue in business terms) as your target for barter. Start trading at the bottom of the range and see if the amount of cash flow you have and the profit you earn is still acceptable. Then try bartering a bit more. Again assess your profit and cash flow. If your numbers are still working out, keep trading until you have reached the maximum level of barter that you want to achieve.

TRADING TIP

Getting started outside of an exchange? Print your business cards with the phrase OPEN TO BARTER or ASK ME ABOUT BARTER. If you've already printed cards, put a little sticker on your cards with the same verbiage. Let your business card smoke out trading partners for you.

CHAPTER 11

BARTER AS A CAREER

While we've focused on getting what you want and need without cash, there is one way to earn money from barter—and that's to work as a barter professional. For more than two decades, that's exactly how Karen earned her living. She worked first in sales for Barter Systems International and then moved into brokering for National Commercial Exchange to get a firm foundation in barter at the ground level. In 1987, she started her own barter company, Trade Resource International, in St. Louis. She operated it until 1995, when she sold it to a national chain that asked her to manage their regional office. She then went on to become the executive director of the International Reciprocal Trade Association, where she got to travel all over the world and meet other barter brokers and exchange owners. Karen has presided over every aspect of bartering, ranging from the detailed account-keeping to the excitement of brokering a million-dollar deal. Bartering allowed Karen to immerse herself in two of the activities she loves most: helping entrepreneurs and connecting people with others who can help them. After so many years in the industry, Karen is, needless to say, a fan of working in barter and the fun and excitement it involves.

Before you consider a career in barter, it helps to understand the culture of the barter world. Although the work atmosphere can differ greatly from brokerage to brokerage—the experience of an employee in Sheboygan will not mirror that of one in Dallas—there are some generalities we can use to describe the industry and what you can anticipate if you work in it.

WORK CULTURE

The trade industry attracts a diverse group of individuals. And when we say individuals, we really mean *individuals*. Many people who are attracted to barter are creative thinkers who like to challenge the status quo and live life their own way. Often, they are mavericks. You will find that there are two primary personality types that populate the industry: those who love to serve others and those who thrive on the adrenaline surge of making the deal. The work is fast paced because deals can evaporate quickly as businesses' needs change.

Some exchanges are like scenes you may have seen on the trading floor of a stock exchange, with people yelling across the room at each other, trying to match barter partners, their blood racing and numbers flying. Other exchanges are quieter, more corporate, less rambunctious. There is very much a sense of "what have you done lately" and people proving their prowess. In this industry, you are evaluated in terms of your last trade. If you made a $1 million deal

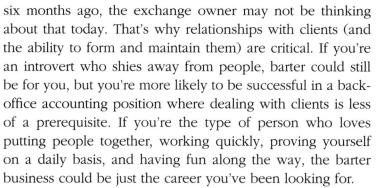

six months ago, the exchange owner may not be thinking about that today. That's why relationships with clients (and the ability to form and maintain them) are critical. If you're an introvert who shies away from people, barter could still be for you, but you're more likely to be successful in a back-office accounting position where dealing with clients is less of a prerequisite. If you're the type of person who loves putting people together, working quickly, proving yourself on a daily basis, and having fun along the way, the barter business could be just the career you've been looking for.

So what kind of careers does barter offer? Quite a varied list. The majority of barter jobs can be found among the 500 or so barter exchanges across the nation. These brokerages ply their trade all the way from small towns to major cities like New York, Chicago, and Los Angeles. As a result, they offer a variety of employment experiences and pay ranges, all based primarily on the size and volume of trades they facilitate. As you might imagine, the larger the exchange, the more opportunities there will be, the higher the pay, and the greater variation in the types of duties employees will be expected to perform. The larger exchanges are more likely to produce more sales so they have more money to pay salaries and benefits like health insurance or retirement savings. Of course, these are generalizations, and there are exceptions, but as an overall rule they hold more weight than not.

Outside of exchanges, there are also major companies that have staffs of brokers who concentrate on specific types of corporate barter deals, ranging from connecting one firm to another to, at the highest levels, working globally to make trades happen between foreign nations for commodities like rice, sugar, or gasoline. There's a bit of everything in between, including positions for accountants and bookkeepers, administrative assistants, sales staff, franchise owners, and more. Let's take a look at some of the most common careers, and then we'll peek at some of the more specialized options, as well.

SALESPERSON

The most common career and the entry point for a lot of barter professionals is being a salesperson or account executive. Starting in sales is a great place to begin because you can then learn a variety of skills that will transfer throughout the industry and make you multifaceted and, therefore, more valuable to an employer. For instance, you will learn how to make cold calls on prospective customers who, perhaps, have never heard of barter. You will also develop a repertoire of answers that will help educate prospective members and overcome their objections to joining an exchange. A natural part of sales is that you will attend a variety of business networking events that will introduce you to company owners. It will be your job to get to know them and build relationships from the ground up that you can turn into new members. That network of contacts and resources will help you get referrals that will produce more sales. Your network will also be invaluable to your broker colleagues, and should you become a broker yourself (more on that in a bit), your network will be a tremendous asset in connecting members who have needs with other members or companies that haven't yet joined the exchange.

Setting your sights on a sales position will enable you to get your foot in the door more quickly than any other aspect of the profession simply because salespeople are always needed and account for the survival of any exchange. Because selling is so essential to a company's survival (any company, truth be told), you may have to stay in sales longer than you initially planned, especially if you develop skill and talent for it. But by having those excellent skills, you become more "layoff proof" and more valuable to your employer.

If you are generating income, you are far less likely to be downsized than if you answer the phones and don't make money for the company. Sales skills also make you a better broker, if you move into that arena. When clients have doubts about bartering (and they often will if they haven't traded in a while or if a trade goes south), you can jump back into sales mode and remind them about the benefits of being a member and the value of bartering. You will need to remind them of all the previous trades they have done and specific items or services that you helped broker for them. Hanging on to a member ensures that you will make more money and will certainly keep the exchange owner in your debt.

Having the great network that you developed as a salesperson will serve you especially well as a broker. The larger your collection of business contacts, the more easily you will be able to put together trades. A strong network also improves your chances of being able to introduce someone you already have a relationship with to a member who can't get what he or she wants from the existing membership. Not only will the member be pleased, but you'll also be able to earn more money by signing up a new member. And of course, all of this will make the boss break into an ear-to-ear grin.

Account executives need to have the same range of job skills that any other salesperson might need, but they also must be patient and willing to educate business owners about barter. If you're a car salesman, you don't need to explain what a car is and what it can do for a customer. But even in the business world, barter is still an activity that requires some explanation, particularly about why the owner would want to do it and how it works. Before you can even begin to have a conversation about a business becoming a member of an exchange, you'll have to work through these education issues.

Another important character trait for a salesperson is being thick-skinned. Just as in any sales position, you'll hear "no" a lot. The best salespeople will tell you that when they first got started, receiving rejection after rejection certainly hurt their feelings and their self-esteem. But what they all eventually figured out is that they couldn't take it personally. Once they made that transition in their thinking, selling became a lot easier and more fruitful.

Personal and business integrity are important traits for an account executive. If you promise a deal, discount, or any other perk to a member, you have to deliver. To overpromise and underdeliver will boomerang back onto you and disappoint the business owner. That can potentially lead to a canceled membership and your new hangout at the unemployment office.

Sometimes as a salesperson, you may be called on to smooth over issues with a member who has become upset for any number of reasons. This is especially true if you have developed a strong relationship with that member and will be more readily able to solve particularly sticky problems like unpaid fees, poor interactions with other members, or inflating prices. The key point to remember here is that just because you sold a membership in the exchange, your responsibility to the member isn't over; in fact, your involvement can be quite vital to the success of the membership over time.

To get into barter membership sales, you don't need previous sales experience, although it certainly helps. Having basic computer skills is a plus. A college education isn't a prerequisite either—just solid sales ability and a willingness to learn how the barter industry works.

Compensation varies greatly by region and is largely based on commissions, with earnings averaging around $60,000 a year. While some sales representatives are paid a salary, most are paid a base salary and commissions that range from 20 percent to 90 percent of the joining fees a new member pays. Part of a salesperson's compensation can come in the form of barter credits that can be used for goods and services within the exchange.

BROKERING AND BEYOND

After the salesperson has brought in a new account, it's time for a broker to get busy making deals happen for the new member. In many ways, the broker is the foundation of the entire exchange. The broker is the glue that cements relationships, proves the value of the membership to the business owner, and financially underpins the entire operation. The broker is the personal face of the exchange after the account executive has sold the membership. A business owner may or may not interact with his or her account executive again but will have weekly or monthly contact with the broker assigned to the company's account. Ultimately, the broker's job is to help clients run their businesses more efficiently, effectively, creatively, and profitably by using barter as a tool.

Every day a broker has to juggle multiple activities, beginning with calling the members on his or her list to see what they need or what problems they are having that the exchange could help solve. Being a broker is about more than just matching a need with a good or service. A broker needs to be a bit of a detective and find out what is truly happening in the business. On the obvious end, a broker needs to find out what goods or services a company needs—but not in general terms. Specifics are important in this job. It's not enough to know that the member needs office paper. The broker needs to know that half of the paper needs to be suitable for a copier and the other half needs to be a mixture of pink, purple, and lime green that will be used for an eye-catching direct-mail campaign. It also has to be deliverable within the time frame that the business owner requires and in the quantities needed.

Price is also a factor. While it's tempting to think that price doesn't matter because a barter deal doesn't automatically involve cash, it actually does (more on that in a bit). Once the broker has located what the member needs, the fun part kicks in—getting to inform the member that you have what he or she needs and can deliver as hoped.

The impact of barter on a business, its employees, and its owners can be dramatic, and the broker plays an essential role in that. For instance, Karen recalls helping a sawmill owner buy advertising that helped publicize the grand opening of the mill's second location. That advertising ensured that the opening was an immense success and brought in business right away. That fast start made all the difference in helping the owner become profitable, pay employees and himself, and be successful.

Another time, Karen was able to help a struggling small-business owner get much-needed orthodontic care for his children that he hadn't been able to afford. At another company, barter paid for an enormous Christmas party each year for the workers. An employee who left to take a job elsewhere told Karen he didn't realize how well treated he had been. He confessed that he missed the special treatment of the big party and year-round goodies like movie tickets, a lending library of books, flowers or other gifts on their anniversary, and bonuses paid in barter credits that could be used for anything the employees wanted. In some cases, employees told Karen that bartered goods or services helped their families survive and thrive, especially at Christmas when a family's entire stash of presents came from bartering through the exchange. Karen wouldn't trade the warm fuzzies she got from those experiences for anything.

The detective work the broker does also comes in handy in other ways. Often a broker who has gotten to know the members well will have a business owner divulge that the company is in trouble because the owner can't pay the bills. In those instances, the broker can come to the rescue. With the business owner's blessing, the broker can contact the companies the owner owes money to and suggest that the bills be paid in barter credits. Maybe the entire bill won't be satisfied, but paying even a part of the outstanding balance with barter credits can free up cash for the member who was in difficulty, helping the business turn a corner and get on more stable footing. Keeping a creditor happy can also keep the business from going bankrupt. (It also means that the broker has just brought a new member into the fold, which will certainly ring up bigger numbers on the cash register for the broker when the next paycheck rolls in.)

Another way a rep can help is by brokering a deal when a member doesn't have enough cash and needs raw materials or supplies that will enable the company to produce more goods or services and bring in more cash. If the broker can supply the needs of a cash-strapped firm on trade, it could mean the difference between employees being paid and the company remaining open. And of course, the new members that come aboard to trade with the existing member will pump up the broker's paycheck.

Brokers also get to flex their advertising and public relations muscles (or discover they have them if they haven't figured that out already). Many are responsible for finding out what members want to sell more of and sending out e-mail blasts promoting those goods and services. Sending out sales promotions are a key part of the job because they not only provide more sales for members but also boost the broker's trade volume and, therefore, bottom line.

In many ways, the broker acts as an auxiliary marketing director for member companies. Few people are seeking to buy lawn furniture in the winter, but the outdoor furniture retailer still needs to make sales in January. By working with the broker, the retailer can promote barter specials like a January sale that could move inventory out of the warehouse and generate credits. Often it's up to the broker to figure out how to put together a promotion and transmit it to the other exchange members; this can even include calling individual members and directly offering the trade. This gets easier if the broker has been proactive and has tracked what sorts of goods and services the member has on his or her wish list. Making individual matches is very much a part of the broker's daily duties.

Paperwork is definitely a significant segment of a broker's job. Maintaining account records, sending out statements of monthly trading activity, and dealing with discrepancies if they arise are part of pushing paper. A certain amount of attention to detail is necessary to perform this part of the job, but it isn't overly burdensome. In larger brokerages, administrative personnel will handle those sorts of duties, freeing the broker to do what he or she does best—make the deals happen.

Brokers also get to play host or hostess with the mostest. Throughout the year, but particularly during holiday shopping seasons, brokers will be responsible for helping to plan and orchestrate mixers, trade fairs, auctions, and the exchange's holiday shopping bazaar—fun events that members look forward to so they can spend some of their credits for personal items and generally fulfill all the requests on their gift lists. It's not uncommon for a member to spend $2,000, $3,000, or more at a holiday party. Brokers will help source special items like a high-end piece of jewelry or state-of-the-art equipment for these events. These are some of the few times a year that brokers are able to see their clients face-to-face, and the atmosphere is usually so joyful that it's just a pleasure for everyone. Karen loved watching the members snap up gifts for their families and employees they might not have been able to afford if they'd had to pay cash. For some members, barter enabled them to provide gifts where they would have had none; for others, barter provided more lavish gifts. In the end, barter allowed the members to provide a great Christmas for their families.

Brokers will occasionally get to put on their teacher hat and help lead a seminar for new members on how to trade, what to expect, and how to maximize their membership. Those sorts of seminars are important for the early success of clients. They are also key to helping produce more earnings for the broker. Once a member understands how the game is played, a broker may ask for a company or store tour so she can learn more about the business and find more opportunities for trading that could help the company boost profits. The best brokers try to absorb as much as possible about all aspects of the firm's operations so they can make as many trade recommendations as possible.

As gratifying as being a broker is, there are downsides, just as in any job. One of the most difficult aspects of a broker's work is determining if the price the seller is charging is appropriate. Some members inflate the price of their goods or services so that they can rack up more barter credits within the exchange. Since a broker isn't intimately familiar with the cost of every single product on the market, it's easy for a member to inflate prices undetected—until there is a complaint. Then it becomes the broker's job to do some competitive price shopping and find out what the marketplace is actually charging for the product or service.

Once the broker has the data in hand, it's time to act. If the price is fair, the broker has to explain that to the member and back it up with the data to prove it. If the price has, in fact, been elevated, the broker will have to go back to the seller and discuss that information. In some cases, the broker will find that the higher price was warranted because of special features, better quality, or other factors. In others, the higher price isn't justifiable, and the broker will have to discuss with the seller and buyer how their accounts will be adjusted to reflect the proper price. If a consistent pattern of price gouging is established, the broker or the exchange owner will have to deliver the bad news that the seller is being evicted from the exchange. Without a doubt, this is one of the least enjoyable aspects of being a broker.

There are times when a member will run up a huge stockpile of debits but isn't selling much. When that happens, the exchange owner may have to put that account on hold. It's the broker's job to inform the member of that unhappy news and to bear the (typically) negative reaction. That can become sticky when the member wants to trade with another member for something important to the business and can't until the hold is lifted. In those moments, the member will question why he or she is a member and want to leave. Others try to bully the broker into returning the account to active status.

These were among the most difficult moments for Karen when she was a broker and then, later, an owner. A broker's natural inclination is to let people trade freely. This not only meets their needs but also benefits the broker's take-home pay. The trick is to help the member execute more sales so the debts can be erased and the company can return to active status. That means the broker will have to work harder to make those sales happen, especially if the goods or services the on-hold member is offering aren't much in demand. As

Karen learned, the broker is responsible *to* the member, not *for* the member.

Brokers are also on the front line of coping with deals gone bad, dealing with members harboring bad feelings, and making everything right. Sound like a tall order? It can be. And it's not rare. Between 10 percent and 20 percent of deals flop each month, for a variety of reasons. When they do, that certainly doesn't make members happy. If they become too discouraged, they'll leave, and then, in the end, the broker's paycheck will take the hit.

What can upset a member? Plenty. When a deal falls apart at the last minute because of price issues, delivery problems, or other factors, the broker will have to try to patch up the match or find another that will satisfy the member left holding the bag. At other times, members will become disgruntled over being treated poorly by another member but won't tell his or her broker. As the grievance festers and the resentment grows, one of two events will occur: The member will quit the brokerage mysteriously, or the broker's ears will take a blistering when the member finally unloads the unhappy tale. Either way, it's up to the broker to assuage bad feelings and, if necessary, lure the member back to the exchange.

The other major downside of being a broker is having to grapple with members who bypass the exchange and make direct trades with other members. Members sign agreements when they join to prohibit that behavior. But the temptation is strong, especially between members who already have executed successful trades together on a repeated basis. Since they know and trust each other, making a direct trade is easier to do, and it enables them to avoid the fees on transactions. When a broker finds out that a direct trade has happened (and he or she doesn't always know when it occurs), he or she will have to alert the exchange owner to the situation. Either the owner or the broker will be faced with reprimanding the member or, most likely, ejecting the company from the exchange. It's never pleasant and can produce tense encounters and long-lasting bad feelings.

So what are some of the key characteristics of a good broker? You must be creative, creative, creative. Did we mention creative? In the cash world, a customer has a need, walks into a business (or clicks over to a Web site), pays with cash or a credit card, and goes away with the good or service needed. But transactions can be much more complicated in the barter world, and they absolutely, positively require much more resourcefulness than a cash deal. You might have to persuade a member who isn't trading at the moment to make a deal for a product that no one else in the network is offering. If you can't keep the trade local and quick, you may have to search within your extended barter network, including national networks, to make a match. You might also put in a call to someone in your network who isn't in the exchange to see if he or she is interested. You could also ask your clients if they can recommend a vendor who could supply the good or service. If all else fails, you might have to make a cold call to companies listed in online business directories that could fill the bill.

Besides being resourceful, brokers need to be flexible. When the usual vendor can't deliver what a member needs, you have to troll your network and search out another vendor who can supply it. You'll also need great customer service skills to keep your list of members happy and trading. In the broker world, you're only as good as your last trade, so being persistent is an excellent personal trait to possess. A desire to help people and a willingness to learn the rudiments of how a business operates and the detailed needs of particular industries are also important. A sense of compassion will also come in quite handy when a business owner is demanding your help. It could be that the trade you help her make is critical to the company's survival and the continued employment of its workers. Being understanding and helpful will take you farther than reacting with frustration or anger toward a stressed-out member who is simply trying to stay afloat.

It might be obvious, but brokers need to be self-starters and highly motivated to facilitate trades. If a large percentage of your pay comes from the fees generated by each trade, you won't make much if you kick back and just expect the deals to happen by themselves. Whether you're introverted or extroverted, it matters not. Both personality types do well in the barter business as long as they can forge good customer relationships and maintain them.

Being a broker gives you an exciting, interesting career to chat about at cocktail parties, church socials, or other gatherings. Karen found that when she met people socially and they asked what sort of work she did, being a barter broker sparked plenty of interest and conversation. People love to hear about deals you've made worth thousands (maybe even millions) of dollars. Now that's stimulating conversation in most any gathering.

A high school education is sufficient to be a broker, although for people with business savvy and an ability to learn, even a high school diploma isn't necessary. If you can balance a checkbook, you've got enough math skills and smarts to be a broker. All of which means that brokering is a job open to plenty of folks who are looking for a career change.

So how much can you earn as a broker? Just like a salesperson, it depends on how large your exchange is and the volume of trades it does monthly. Compensation is pegged to a base salary and commission on the fees paid by members on each trade. Sometimes the commission comes out of just the sell side of the trade, sometimes the buy side, and sometimes both. Every exchange is different. Generally speaking, a broker's income ranges from $30,000 to $50,000 a year. More or less is certainly possible given the circumstances and level of motivation of the broker. A portion of compensation can also include barter credits. Those are often the source of performance bonuses brokers will receive for a job well done.

SPECIALTY BROKERS

For brokers who want to specialize beyond general business-to-business trades, there are particular industries that demand industry-specific knowledge to make trades. Specialty traders focus on areas such as travel, media trades, and corporate barter. While the barter industry doesn't issue certifications for these types of specialties, there are companies that employ teams of these brokers and have their own education programs. To work as a specialty trader, you'll have to demonstrate your knowledge of bartering and a fundamental understanding of the industry you wish to specialize in. For instance, if you want to go into media trades, you'll need to have a background in media and show that you grasp the lingo, what drives those types of trades, and what the clients who want to purchase media time need. Since there are no college courses or workshops that teach specialty trading, all of the knowledge has to be acquired on the job before you can move deeper into these careers.

Perhaps one of the most compelling aspects of specialty barter is that these positions can pay more than general barter or can satisfy a particular desire or passion on the trader's part. Let's take a closer look.

Travel Barter

In some large exchanges, brokers will become expert in helping clients book cruises, hotels, meeting space in other cities, vacation rentals, and much more. Those brokers can go on to parlay that experience into working with larger and more-complex travel trades. Some even opt to work exclusively in travel barter. Take Mark Knudson of Seattle as an example.

Mark began as a general barter broker three decades ago but was so enamored of traveling that he began to focus more and more on that. In time, he hung out his own shingle for travel barter. Because Mark speaks Spanish and enjoys travel throughout Mexico, he began to specialize in bartering hotel rooms in that country. It also helped that Mexican culture is far more accepting of barter than those of many other countries. Mark's job is to chat up hoteliers in Mexico and persuade them to supply him with a block of rooms and a certain number of nights in those rooms. In return, he trades a variety of services, ranging from those he offers directly—such as video production, graphic design, and magazine stories on a particular hotel in travel or specialty magazines—to credits he has earned through other exchanges. Because Mark has a long history in the general barter industry, he also can trade credits he has earned from existing barter networks and exchanges; about half his credits are traded this way. A quarter is traded in direct barter for his services or hotel room inventory, and he sells the remainder for cash. He handles thousands of barter transactions a year.

Mark readily admits that this is a tough specialty and not for the faint of heart. In truth, you should plan on being self-employed if you want to pursue this career. Self-employment entails a big income risk compared with being an employee of an exchange. As an entrepreneur, you won't be guaranteed an income unless you can generate sales. The upside is that your income is determined by you, not the boss. A travel barter broker could earn $80,000 a year or more. But if she's terrible at it or starting with no experience or connections, it could be closer to zero.

To get started in this specialty, make sure you have a firm understanding of general barter. It certainly helps to be a member of a trade exchange, and it also will serve you well to have plenty of connections in the business. You'll be able to turn those connections and your travel goods or services into items you can use. To extract cash, you'll need to be clever about how you can sell your travel inventory for dollars.

Some of the personality traits that go well with this type of specialty are a love of travel, a high degree of attention to detail, tremendous flexibility, creativity in making deals, a strong work ethic, leadership skills, sales ability, and absolute trust that what you have to trade is valuable. A high school education will be sufficient for this profession, but a good business sense and ability to adhere to sound business principles will be important for success.

Media Broker

One of the more-demanding barter professions is being a media broker. For this career, you'll need an excellent understanding of purchasing in quite an array of media outlets. You'll have to be an expert in buying advertising in newspapers and magazines; on radio, TV, cable, Web sites, and billboards; for in-store promotions; and much more.

At one time, being a media broker brought the same sort of reaction as being a used-car salesman. That was due, in large part, to media not having to do much bartering. But as the media landscape has changed and become more competitive, bartering is becoming more widely appreciated because of the clients it can produce. In addition, clients need their media buys to be profitable despite an explosion of competition from more and more sources, like the Internet. The good news is that as barter has become incorporated into an increasing number of media buys, brokers and barter have become more acceptable and, finally, welcomed.

Media brokers—also called media market specialists—work for barter companies as well as firms that specialize in bartering a client company's assets for media time. If you work for a local or regional barter exchange, chances are good that you'll be brokering other deals along with handling media buys for members. At the corporate media-buying level, these specialists typically have particular media that they are familiar with buying advertising from, including spot TV ads, radio time, local or national TV, the Internet, consumer or trade magazines, and much more. The reason these professionals specialize within media brokering is because it's such a complex industry.

Before you can reach this demanding level of employment, you'll most likely work as an assistant or a coordinator or similar support position within the media-buying department. These are entry-level or early-stage career positions that are the lower rungs of the ladder that leads to top-level media buying. They are a great way for someone who loves communications and business to build a career that has barter at its foundation.

Probably one of the most enjoyable elements of being a media specialist is the haggling involved. The media specialist's job is focused on getting the best placement and/or largest number of ads possible for the client. Excellent negotiation skills are a must. Since all barter media buys are going to be a combination of trade and cash, buyers have to be very savvy. They have to know what the client's goals are with the media plan and achieve them, often to the tune of millions of dollars. In the process they are guaranteed to interact with some quirky characters and people with high-energy, plain-spoken personalities. This is a world that moves fast, cuts high-end deals, and doesn't mince words. If wheeling and dealing is something you thrive on, this is your kind of life. It's certainly not for introverts, the timid, or those who can't push for what they need.

A media broker also needs to be patient and able to work with many different mass communication outlets at the same time to make an entire media barter plan come to fruition. It helps to be able to see all the individual parts of the puzzle while at the same time envisioning what the entire plan must look like in order to meet the client's advertising and promotion goals.

The difficult elements of this job are the details and pace. Buying ad space in or on hundreds of newspapers, radio stations, TV stations, billboards, Web sites, and multiple other venues requires having a deep knowledge of advertising rates, which cities are and aren't right for the client's ads, and which media are well suited to the product or service (and those that aren't) and keeping intricate records of what was bought, when the ads will run, and where they will be seen or heard.

At the highest levels, pay is good for these types of jobs. However, since most of the corporate media broker positions are located in and around New York City, the cost of living is high, and that eats up a lot of those high wages. At the entry level, a media broker's assistant could be paid $30,000 a year. The range rises dramatically for the media specialists, beginning at around $55,000 annually and rising to nearly $90,000 a year. Some firms pay bonuses based on performance as well.

Media brokers need to have either a bachelor's degree in communications, business, or a related field or significant experience in the barter industry. A college degree is definitely necessary if you have no barter experience and are just entering the workforce. Most corporate barter firms are more interested in hiring degreed professionals for entry-level jobs and training them on the intricacies of barter and media rather than hiring seasoned barter professionals. But each company and position varies, so it pays to research the position and figure out what skills you have that will translate into experience or qualities that could be useful to the company. Ultimately, you'll never know what might have occurred unless you apply for a job you're interested in.

Barter Consultant

Those who are highly experienced in the trade industry have another barter profession to consider—barter consultant. Consultants are experts at bartering between companies. While they certainly know how to barter for their personal needs, their work is focused on helping small to large firms make strategic trades that will help solve a variety of problems or create new opportunities. Those trades can be as simple as brokering a deal to upgrade computer software for an entire engineering division to brokering a multifaceted trade that involves millions of dollars of unused inventory, vehicles, a corporate jet, or real estate.

The challenge for barter consultants is to first find companies that will contract with them for their services. Then, the consultant must analyze the most effective barter opportunities, educate the company on how the trades will happen, and make sure that the company gets a fair return on what it receives in trade. When you are in charge of millions of dollars worth of products, perhaps even hundreds of millions of dollars you really have to be at the top of your barter game. That's the job of a consultant.

Great consultants think of what they do as an art form, and because of the complexity of the trades, that's certainly true. Instead of trading with one partner, a consultant might be executing scores of trades with just as many partners, depending on what is being bartered and who is involved.

Consultants have to be skilled at creative thinking, and they have to be entrepreneurs, since they aren't permanent employees of any company. They also must be highly motivated, good at listening to clients' needs, and excellent at follow-up and managing details.

One of the many upsides of this demanding career is being self-employed (if you're the type of person who enjoys being your own boss and taking risks) and having constant change in your work life. You'll work for a wide variety of companies and industries, so you can't get comfortable in just one line of business. There is also the thrill of making a deal, developing relationships with trading partners, negotiating, and meeting new people constantly. This is definitely a job for extroverts. Shrinking violets need not apply.

A college education isn't necessary to become a consultant, but a thorough understanding of how business-to-business barter works is essential. For nearly every consultant, that means either having owned a barter exchange or having worked in one at the broker level and beyond.

Compensation is completely determined by how aggressive the consultant is in sales and rounding up new companies to consult with. You could earn a few thousand dollars a year as a sideline or six figures from brokering large corporate trades, of which you get a percentage. What you make is entirely up to you and your moxie in this career.

TRADE EXCHANGE OWNER

Being an exchange owner combines the best of being a salesperson, broker, and entrepreneur. Like any entrepreneur, if you are the owner of an exchange, you get to call all the shots, make all the decisions, reap all the rewards, and take all the risk. Being an entrepreneur takes a stout heart, money (in some cases), time, persistence, and either a thorough knowledge of the barter industry or a willingness to learn it. Many exchange owners became the head honcho after working their way up from other barter positions such as salesperson, broker, and even administrative assistant. That's one of the beauties of this industry: It's open to all sorts of people, especially those with drive and the ability to work hard.

You already know how a barter exchange works, but what you may not realize is that there are two basic types of general business-to-business exchanges: independent and franchised/licensed. Which type of exchange you start will depend on how fat your wallet is and how ornery you are. If you are quite an independent thinker, are not prone to following somebody else's rules, like to figure things out as you go, and don't have much cash, starting an independent exchange would be a better fit for you. If you like having a map of how to do things, have several thousand dollars to invest, can easily follow someone else's rules and regula-tions, and prefer to have support and advice on what you are attempting, purchasing a barter exchange franchise or license is a great option for you.

Independent exchanges are started from the ground up by individuals who want to be in control of every aspect of the business. The start-up costs on this type of exchange are less because you don't have to pay a franchise or license fee to the corporation that sells those rights. But you also give up the knowledge (including lessons learned from mistakes), training, and support that the franchisor provides, so there's a big trade-off to consider. The other financial factor in being an independent exchange is that you won't have to pay any ongoing fees to a franchise corporation. All the profits you earn go straight into your own pocket (after you've covered your expenses like office, staff, computers, software, etc.).

Franchised or licensed exchanges begin with more support and instruction from the corporation that sells the franchise or license to open the business under its logo. The business will operate in much the same way as an independent exchange, but you'll have to pay a substantial amount for use of the license or franchise ($20,000 for ITEX, for example), along with a percentage of your profits. What you get for your money is a recognizable brand name, training on how to operate the exchange, a network of brokers in other cities you can trade with, and help from the corporate staff with your questions and problems. You also typically receive a thick training manual that explains all the procedures, software for trading, all accounting provided for you, opportunities to attend industry conventions, conference calls to discuss issues, and (for those that provide them) matching funds for advertising purchases. You will have to follow the rules and procedures as well as keep your fees paid, or you'll run afoul of the corporation. Your sales volume will have to be strong enough to pay those fees. So while the coaching and support are helpful, they come at a cost that shoestring budgets may not be able to handle.

What you'll need to get started in both situations is a computer and either a home or a commercial office space, a phone, business cards, a logo and company name, stationery, barter software, a fast Internet connection, and the proper city, county, and state businesses licenses. You may also need employees if you have the money to pay them and a salesperson or an ability to sell.

How much can you earn as an exchange owner? That depends completely on how successful you are at selling the exchange to new members, facilitating trades that generate fees, satisfying clients so they stay in the fold, and keeping your expenses low. If you can't do those things, you may lose money. That's the high-risk element of being an entrepreneur, and it's one that you should consider before taking the leap into business ownership.

BARTER CLUB OWNER

Some traders are choosing to start their own barter clubs, which is similar to being an owner of a commercial barter exchange. These are organizations that can be quite loose or very formal, depending on the aims, energy, investment, and motivations of the founder. We make a distinction between a barter club and a commercial barter exchange simply based on how the club is organized, whether it charges fees, and if it is focused on individuals more so than companies. Clubs are certainly not franchised by the national barter exchanges such as ITEX and are more likely to charge lower fees, forego membership contracts, or have a particular focus. Sometimes they are nonprofits aimed at helping eliminate financial stress or poverty for their members. Alternatively, some are just intended to let members have fun bartering.

At the least-organized level of a barter club, a founder or group of people with similar interests will come together to trade. The group could be stay-at-home moms, doll collectors who want to expand their collections or buy clothes and accessories, gearheads itchy to swap car paraphernalia, or a social group in a particular town that just enjoys spending time together. These folks gather at regular times, perhaps monthly or bimonthly, and trade face-to-face. The bartering is loose, and the vibe is social and easygoing.

Meetup.com provides a great venue for starting a club, attracting members, and communicating with them. One that we like was started by Betsy Thurman, a Minneapolis, Minnesota, nurse who just wanted to help people who were struggling financially. Her Meetup barter club evolved after members of another group she belongs to suggested they wanted to barter. So Betsy got busy and started the barter club. She invited members from the original group to join, posted announcements in the barter section of CraigsList.org, and asked those who joined to invite others. The growth was slow, but as it happened, members began trading all sorts of goods and services—anything from carpet laying to produce. Betsy organizes social activities such as a bowling night so that members can meet, get to know each other better, and have fun. When the members become more familiar with each other, they are more likely to trade.

That's the same approach Steve McNulty took when he began including barter as part of the Triangle Area Homesteaders group he founded on Meetup.com in Wake Forest, North Carolina. Homesteaders are individuals who want to rediscover ways to be self-sufficient and less reliant on grocery stores, utilities, and other vendors. They share knowledge and skills—often lesser-known arts like weaving, animal husbandry, or beekeeping—to become more self-sustaining. Barter for this group became a necessity in some respects. For example, when many members are raising chickens, there tend to be a lot of people with excess eggs. The same is true for those who garden or raise bees for honey. So Steve started holding bartering meetings to allow those with excess goods to trade with each other. It's common to see members trading tomatoes for homemade soap, or eggs for fresh milk.

If you've got the urge to launch your own Meetup barter group, there are a couple of strategies you should know about that will help you attract members and get them trading once you do. First, get the word out by, of course, forming your group on Meetup and asking some of your friends to join. At the same time, put notices of your group on CraigsList under your town's barter section. It's free, easy, and effective. Even if you have only a handful of members at first, hold a meeting so that everyone can get to know each other and start to form friendships if they haven't done so already.

Combining your meeting with some other social activity is a great idea since it gives people a reason to interact and chat. A swap meet right off the bat is perfect, certainly, but another activity that just helps people become buddies before they start trading could help improve the flow of trades initially. Bowling, a card game, a nature walk, a baseball game or other sports outing, or any other activity that encourages people to interact are ideas to consider. Name tags, as cheesy as they might seem, are a great way to help people get over the jitters and introduce themselves. And as the host, try to introduce people to each other, welcome those you don't know, and match up people who might have similar interests.

One caution is that depending on the diversity of your group, you may have to act as a sort of moderator for the group. Since you'll be acquiring members from across a wide area, even if you live in a small town, you may find that some people have divergent or extreme views compared to the majority. In other cases political ideology or religious proselytizing could crop up. Those sorts of strong opinions can cause members who don't think the same way to feel uncomfortable. It's up to you to speak with the individual who is expressing an extreme perspective and request that he or she stop. If the person continues, you'll have to ask him or her to leave the group or risk losing many other traders you've worked hard to bring into the fold. It's an unpleasant job, but it can be made easier if you post a policy against expressing religious, political, or ideological opinions at meetings or on group forums, message boards, and group e-mail. When you make clear what the policy is from the start, you'll run into fewer problems later.

By the same token, if you find people who are consistently cheating at trades, inflating their trade values, or acting unethically, you will have to be the one to ask them to leave the group. Again, announcing a policy against such behavior whenever a new person joins the group will save you aggravation and stress down the road.

Many of these same principles apply to the next type of barter organization we'll discuss—formal barter clubs. These are typically for-profit companies that are less structured than a commercial barter exchange and primarily offer trades over a Web site. After the economy soured, more of these clubs started popping up as barter-minded people looked for ways to help each other cope with less in their paychecks or no paycheck at all. An added benefit is that they help build community. When you trade with strangers, you get to know them and develop a shared history, and soon they're no longer strangers.

The founders of these clubs are entrepreneurs, either intentional or accidental, so they quickly have to learn business skills if they don't have them already. They also discover that they need help. A lawyer, a Web site designer, a graphic designer, an accountant, and, quite often, salespeople are necessary to get the operation up and running. Software, which can cost $1,300 or more, is also necessary to track trades efficiently and keep members up-to-date on their trade balances.

Once the club's Web site is active, the founders will have to promote it like their life depended on it (and sometimes it does if they've taken out a second mortgage or borrowed heavily to pay for the start-up). That means going to lots of meetings, community groups, networking sessions, and other events to talk up the club. Being an extrovert (or having the ability to be one when necessary) is important. If you aren't one when you start such a club, you'll get the benefit of developing that skill, or you'll need to find a partner who can be the public face of the organization.

Barter clubs usually charge members a small fee to join, about $15 to $50 annually, with businesses usually paying toward the higher end of the fee range. The club might also want a percentage of the value of the trade, but that requirement isn't always present. It just depends on how altruistic the founders want to be or how deeply in debt they became to form the club.

Starting a business, even a laid-back barter club, is a big job and not for the slow moving and unmotivated. You'll also need to be a risk taker and (mostly) unafraid of failure. We're not saying we think you'll fail; far from it. But this is a large undertaking, and you must be ready for a lot of hard work.

The compensation for this type of work, like anything entrepreneurial, depends solely on how well you bring new members into the club and how well you keep them in the fold. If you are able to do that and keep your costs low, you'll be more likely to be successful and earn a tidy living. You'll enjoy meeting all those new traders and introducing them to the thrilling world of barter and the chase of the next great trade.

LIFE OF A BROKER

Terry Brandfass has been a barter broker for more than thirty years. She started as a broker with BXI and eventually became a broker and owner with ITEX Corporation in Phoenix and Tucson, Arizona. Before she became a broker, Terry had worked in the hotel and restaurant industry, but she quickly grew bored. She needed more stimulation, and when she discovered bartering, she knew it was the path for her.

Terry has been hooked on the barter industry for three decades because she enjoys the variety in each day, and she loves making deals happen. She often starts her day by chatting with clients over the phone to see what challenges they are facing, what products or services their business requires, and how the exchange can help.

When a client says he or she needs something, filling that need becomes like a game of hide-and-seek. Part of the game is understanding *exactly* what the business needs and what it has to offer in exchange. It's not enough to know that the company does printing. Terry has to know exactly what kind of printing the company can produce (small jobs, large offset printing runs, packaging products, etc.); then she has to get a grasp of what the printer lacks. If the company needs a new ink supplier, she has to determine if it can be any printing ink or if it must be soy ink. Those sorts of details are essential to making a barter match and keeping clients happy. She also enjoys using barter to help members move their excess inventory, find clients for their services, or fill unused manufacturing capacity. When she can help a client collect on an unpaid invoice, that excites both Terry and the client.

One of the most rewarding aspects of her job is keeping an entrepreneur in business, especially when it appears that nearly all is lost. Terry has worked with many members who have been forced into bankruptcy court. Judges and attorneys don't understand barter and its power, so Terry has to educate them and help facilitate trades with vendors the business owes money to so that the debts can be reduced.

Another part of her job is creating the flyers that her brokerage sends out, announcing new members who have joined the exchange, deals and promotions, and upcoming events. Making up those flyers means she has had to master some basic desktop publishing techniques along with managing an e-mail database of members. She also attends the events she promotes and helps introduce members to one another. When the members are friends, Terry has found that barter relationships are stronger, trades are fairer, and more trades happen—all good news for her, since more trades mean a bigger paycheck.

One of the most tedious elements of her job is having to check prices when members complain that they paid too much. Not only must she do comparison-shopping herself, but she also must check with other members who have used the business being criticized to see what their experience was and how much they were charged. Figuring out if a price was inflated on services can be especially difficult because an apples-to-apples comparison might not be possible. No matter what, she has to respond to the member's concerns, which can be tough if price gouging has, in fact, occurred.

Because Terry gets to know her members and their buying habits so well, she becomes more than just their broker. They talk with her about all sorts of business problems, and she works hard to try to solve those issues, sometimes exercising her most creative muscles to do it. As the friendships deepen, her role sometimes becomes one of emotional support; she becomes a sounding board, confidante, and general problem solver. It's a role she enjoys and, she concedes, not what most people would expect when they think of brokering business deals. But since running a business is quite an emotion-filled endeavor for the majority of entrepreneurs, Terry isn't surprised at how her job has evolved over the years.

While plenty of brokers work nine-to-five days, Terry feels like her success directly correlates to being flexible with how much time she invests in the job. While some of her weeks might be only thirty hours, others can be fifty hours. It all depends on what the members need and how much extra effort she puts into fulfilling their business needs. Many brokers will hand three vendor names to a member who calls looking for something. But Terry's secret is digging a little deeper to see if the vendor has exactly what the member wants, if the price is right, and if the product or service can be delivered when and how the member needs it. That extra bit of work might mean she works a few nights or handles member calls on the weekend. But in the final analysis, Terry feels that this sort of detailed service increases her clients' volume and their satisfaction with the exchange and is what distinguishes her career from others. And that gives her joy in a job well done.

TRADING TIP

If you want to cinch a job in the barter industry, make sure you've done some direct trades so you can tell your prospective boss about your great bartering ability. Having a few successful "war stories" will show that you understand barter, you like to negotiate, and you are expanding your skills.

TRADING TIP

No matter whether you want to be a trade broker, own an exchange, or just start your own barter club, it helps to study up on marketing strategies. We're fans of Jay Conrad Levinson's book *Guerrilla Marketing*.

CHAPTER 12

BARTER TO YOUR HEALTH!

Without a doubt, the single most pressing barter want that we've encountered in recent years is the need for health care. Because so many Americans lack health insurance, they are looking for any avenue that enables them to afford medical care. And it's not only medical doctors that people are seeking; dental care is just as much in demand. The need runs the gamut from psychological care to chiropractic to physical therapy. We sympathize with the plight of those who have physical or emotional issues but lack the money to afford the care that would restore them to health. Barter, while not a panacea, can help and, as you'll see, can even be a lifesaver.

First, let's clear up a misperception: Doctors, psychologists, psychiatrists, and dentists are not prohibited from bartering with patients (with one exception that we'll explore in a moment). Nor is bartering considered unethical, as some people believe. Barter is permitted to all members of the medical profession. The exception to this rule is that barter is prohibited under federal law for patients whose care is paid for by Medicare or Medicaid. Providers are not allowed to waive co-payments or deductibles or receive services or items below the fair market value for medical services provided to those on Medicare or Medicaid. Providers who violate this rule could pay up to $10,000 per violation.

The only ethical restriction is in cases where a medical professional uses the barter relationship to pressure a patient into some sort of payment or action he or she wouldn't normally be expected to do. Generally speaking, since barter relationships are more involved or engaged than those based solely on cash, your interactions with a health-care practitioner are more personal. This could give a provider an insight into a patient's personal weakness and, therefore, an advantage in dealing with you, for good or for bad.

For instance, suppose you were bartering with a psychologist for counseling to help you deal with feelings of childhood abandonment. The psychologist, if he was unethical, might threaten to stop working with you if you didn't pay more for your sessions than he normally charges. He would be exploiting your fears of abandonment by threatening to stop counseling you unless you overpay. This sort of behavior is prohibited by the American Psychological Association as unethical. That doesn't mean the pressure is illegal or would necessarily result in any sort of condemnation by the APA or regulators, but it is against the APA's code of ethical conduct, and the counselor shouldn't do it. Of course, we believe these manipulations are rare and easily avoided by having a clear agreement between the counselor and client/ patient on how the barter arrangement will work. Nonetheless, we wanted to provide an example of how barter could be abused so that people can avoid these situations, rare as they may be.

If you've attempted to barter for health care already, you know how frustrating it can be to strike a deal. It helps to understand why that is the case. Although the reasons are numerous, they can be overcome with some persistence and by taking the time to seek out the right trading partner.

For a variety of reasons, health-care professionals prefer not to deal with people whom they haven't treated before. They are fearful that a patient approaching them without cash or any sort of history with the practice may not live up to his or her end of the barter arrangement. If you fail to make good on your end of the trade, a doctor or dentist will certainly have lost time caring for you when she could have been treating a paying patient instead. This is especially true of physicians, who typically see a different patient every five to seven minutes in today's ultra-fast-paced office environments.

Health-care professionals are also afraid they might lose cash on your care for services they have to pay for, such as laboratory work, diagnostic tests, or other services that are ordered through their offices and for which they bill you. These are hard costs that the provider must reimburse versus time spent in the office. They also worry that the trade will be uneven, and they won't be able to justify receiving less in trade than a cash payment would produce, considering their fixed costs (i.e., paying their staff, professional fees, continuing education, rent, utilities, etc.).

Along the same lines, they fret that the value of what they are being offered in trade won't be obvious or easily discernible on the open market, and, therefore, they won't be fairly compensated. Others worry that they'll be flooded with patients who have heard that they barter and become upset when the provider doesn't want to trade. Like any other

GREAT TRADE!

When Eren Hernandez of Reno, Nevada, realized that her boyfriend, Gilberto Carrasco, hadn't been to see a doctor for a physical in five years, she urged him to go to a doctor. The only problem was that Gilberto didn't have health insurance and couldn't afford the cost of coverage or a doctor visit. Eren wasn't put off one bit. A longtime trader and self-proclaimed "trade expert," Eren persueded Gilberto, who co-owns Dr. Feelgood Auto Repair with Eren, to begin trading his auto mechanic skills through the local ITEX barter exchange.

Gilberto agreed, and soon he was getting a full checkup from Dr. Quinn Pauly, a family physician who began accepting trades to increase the number of patients in his practice. Dr. Pauly discovered that Gilberto had an enlarged prostate, so he sent him to see a specialist, who also agreed to trade with the couple. Lab tests confirmed that Gilberto had prostate cancer. Happily, the tests had detected the cancer early, and Gilberto received surgery to remove his prostate and treatment that cured his cancer. Without getting treatment, Gilberto would have died in five years, the doctors told them.

Eren estimates that Gilberto received about $7,000 in treatment through trade, treatment he wouldn't have been able to afford otherwise. Eren gives full credit to barter for providing her boyfriend with access to doctors and treatment that saved his life.

Since then, Eren has been trading like a house afire. She gets veterinary care for her pets and dental care for her father, who was in pain and needed $7,000 in teeth replacements but had no dental insurance. Her next big project was moving their auto repair/auto detailing business across the street and into a new building. She bartered for excavation with a company that she persuaded to join ITEX so she could trade with it. She also traded for architectural design, plumbing, and painting for the new building—easily $10,000 in services. Eren even uses trade for all of the Christmas gifts she gives. Her friends, family, and employees receive much nicer gifts because of barter, and Eren gets to enjoy the holidays a lot more without having to worry about how to pay for it all.

business, cash is essential to survival, and medical professionals have to make sure enough greenbacks flow through the till, or they risk failure.

Some providers place barter patients in the category of low-reimbursement patients, such as those who are covered by the federal- and state-funded Medicaid program that covers low-income individuals. They view those sorts of patients as having multiple medical issues that will require an abundance of their time to treat, which takes them away from cash- or insurance-covered patients. They also wrongly assume that those same patients will resist following "doctor's orders," known as patient compliance, and making the necessary lifestyle changes or following prescribed treatments that would result in healing or improved health.

Finally, many physicians, dentists, and other providers simply have never heard of barter and don't understand how it works. Or if they have heard of it, they don't want to be hassled with figuring it out or burdening their office managers with it.

We don't tell you all of this to scare you off; quite the opposite. We believe that once you understand health-care professionals' perceptions of barter, you will be in a better position to educate them (if necessary) and begin having a conversation that will allay their fears and lead to a deal. And remember: Not all doctors, dentists, and physical therapists are spooked by barter; many embrace it—and we give them an enthusiastic thumbs-up for that!

So how do you get started trading for health care? Here are some ideas and approaches to try. Use these as a jumping-off point and adapt them to your own specific situation and the type of health-care practice you are approaching.

One of the strongest positions to be in to approach a barter proposition is if you already have an existing relationship with a provider. If you have had some sort of treatment in the past, although not necessarily recently, you'll be better served to approach that doctor, dentist, or provider. (We'll address new providers or those you don't have any relationship with in a moment.)

It's best to discuss the possibility of barter directly with the provider rather than a nurse, assistant, or office manager. Your strongest chances will be with a physician, orthodontist, or other professional who owns her own practice. Just as bartering with any sort of business is easier if it's independently owned rather than being a chain, the same rule applies to medical care. If a physician owns his own practice rather than a hospital owning it, you'll be talking to the head honcho, the decision maker, the boss. He doesn't have to check with his office manager, supervisor, or corporate headquarters before deciding to barter. So, clearly, your chances of working out a trade shoot up enormously when there's no outside individual who can scuttle the deal without even hearing your offer.

Some people wait until they've been seen by the provider and the bill is due before they begin the barter conversation. That's a dangerous strategy to try. You're betting that your lack of cash will make the provider more open to "getting paid" via barter versus getting nothing at all or having to accept multiple cash payments. We tend to think of this on a par with your boss coming to you on payday and saying, "Well, we're a little short in Accounting this week, so we're offering to pay you in widgets from the factory." Widgets won't pay your bills (unless you can tap the super-top-secret hidden widget market to cash them out). Since you wouldn't like being manhandled that way at work, we don't recommend it at the dentist's office. Barter works best when the Golden Rule is in full effect.

A better strategy is to call your doctor before making an appointment and speaking to her directly. Explain if you have a situation that particularly calls for barter. Perhaps life has thrown you a curveball, and you need to barter because you have lost your job or gone through a divorce or some other hardship has severely restricted your cash. Offer to pay your bill in full with barter. Be prepared to educate her about what barter is and inform her that it is perfectly legal and ethical. Have on hand a list of as many goods or services you have available in your arsenal to make the trade.

But perhaps most important of all, listen. Lots of people approach a trade, especially one they really need, without asking what the other person is interested in. Oftentimes, people are so intent on discussing what they can offer that they just plain forget to start with the basics and ask what the other person's range of needs is. You might be surprised. While you're busy offering up your list and exercising your jaws, your ears should be getting the biggest workout. You could run through your list or offer your one excellent possibility and discover that none of those options interest your partner. But if you start with finding out what your partner wants, you may stumble onto a great trade, and possibly one that's even easier than you imagined. Simply remain receptive to a range of barter choices.

Once you and the health-care professional settle on what you have to offer, be very clear on what services you will receive. For instance, if you are getting treatment in a doctor's office, ask about laboratory blood work or other diagnostic tests that might be required. Those services could mean additional costs that aren't included in your trade and will have to be paid for in cash, most likely to a lab or other provider who is separate from your physician. It's far better to clear up any confusion at the beginning of the trade than at the back end, when miscommunication could spark bad feelings that will fester and cut you off from future bartering for more services. By the same token, make sure you hold up your end of the bargain. If you receive only one or two office visits and then fail to supply what you offered in trade, you'll guarantee yourself no more treatment, and you'll also ruin potential barter prospects for other patients, whose care could mean the difference between life and death.

What if you don't have a relationship with the medical professional you need? There's still another path to barter success. Ask a close family member or dear friend who goes to this practice to help you—preferably, one who is in good standing with the care provider (i.e., has current or paid account balances). Ideally you'd get a referral from a relative who has been seeing that provider for many years; perhaps even generations of your family have been cared for by this person. Call his office and tell the receptionist that you were referred by your friend or family member. Then ask to speak to the provider about the care you need. Some providers prefer to receive barter requests in a letter, so you might ask the staff if they know which is preferred for that office. Whichever form you use, make sure you reference your relationship to the friend or relative when you communicate to the doctor or other professional. The front-desk employee may not remember to pass along the referral, but it's key to beginning the barter conversation.

Explain what sort of care you are seeking, and ask if he would be willing to consider barter, especially since your friend/relative spoke so highly of him. The idea here, if it isn't already obvious, is that the provider will recognize a referral from a good patient and be more open to working with you so that he can keep that patient. The impact of this sort of approach is even stronger if there are multiple family members under the provider's care. No dentist wants to lose an entire family of patients (especially gum-chomping, candy-loving kids), so your proposal will get a warmer reception and more serious consideration than if you called without a referral.

If you don't have a family member or friend already receiving the type of care from the professional you need, all is not lost. Find a list of the providers who meet your criteria and determine which one (or ones) have been in practice just a short time—maybe only a year or two. You can find that information from a variety of sources: checking the Internet; calling hospital referral services; reviewing the list of professionals who have been licensed most recently by state agencies, such as dental, physical therapy, and healing arts boards; or contacting local and national professional associations such as the American Medical Association, your city's dental society, and others.

If all those avenues fail, call the office of the provider you are interested in and ask how long she has been practicing. If the main provider has been plying her trade for many years, ask if there is a newer member of the staff or one who has recently joined. Chances are good that this provider has a low patient load because she hasn't been in business very long and will be more eager to consider the idea of bartering. When an entrepreneur, even a doctor, is just starting a business, she'll have to be a bit more creative than the old-timers. You can take advantage of that willingness to try something new.

Here's a script you could use to broach the subject of barter with a new clinician:

> *I'd really like to do business with you because I've heard such good things about you. Because of my current situation, I don't have a lot of money, but I really need this care. [Explain what your situation is if it's helpful: job loss, divorce, house burned, etc.]*

> *I'm trying to be creative with how I make payments and settle my bills. Would you be open to barter? If you are, I would be happy to be a referral for you so*

*that you could build your practice faster. I can also
explain more about what barter is and what I have
access to or could provide directly.*

MAKING YOUR CASE

For many health-care professionals, particularly those who
work in highly regulated professions such as physicians and
dentists, the idea of barter may be unheard of or considered
rare. In those cases you'll have to do some educating and be
politely persistent. If you get some push back to the idea of
barter, here are some points to make that might help you sail
past objections.

Explain that doctors and other care providers have been
bartering since the profession was still using saws, candles,
and leeches. Physicians, for instance, used to make house calls
and often got paid in poultry, vegetables, livestock, or some
other good. The practice was common and quite standard
and, as she will discover, still has a useful place today. Reassure her that it isn't illegal or unethical as long as the provider
doesn't try to use inside knowledge or take unfair advantage of the barter relationship. Providers who care for Medicare or Medicaid patients—those who are covered by federal
and state programs that pay for care—are not permitted to
overcharge beyond standard rates. (This is particularly true
for Medicare patients.) Simply put, the doctor will have to
adhere to the practice's normal charges.

Since all health-care providers, at least those who own
their own practices, are businesspeople, you can help your
case by laying out the business advantages of bartering with
you. Those advantages are big. Barter can help the provider
bring in many new patients and grow the practice much
quicker. It happens through barter patients like you who start

GREAT TRADE!

When you live in a rural area, the choice for all sorts of businesses and services shrinks markedly because of the smaller population. That's certainly true for health care. Rural areas are especially short of doctors, dentists, and other health-care providers that you find in abundance in big cities. That's part of the reason Dr. Sharon P. Osborne, an osteopathic physician, decided to move her medical practice from Richmond, Virginia, to Floyd, Virginia. Dr. Osborne is a big believer in the power of barter to alleviate economic difficulty for lower-income patients, and she wanted to make barter a payment option within her medical practice. She suspected that she would have more chances to barter and be able to serve a greater need if she moved back to her rural hometown at the edge of the Blue Ridge Mountains—and her hunch was right.

About 10 percent of her practice at the Barter Clinic pays in trade. She has received a wide array of goods and services in barter, including child care, fruits, vegetables, clothing, firewood, violin lessons, and more. The clinic also accepts community service as trade. Patients can volunteer to help elderly patients or work for community groups in exchange for medical care.

Before accepting a trade, her staff do a bit of research to determine the value of the good or service. This gives them an idea of how much of the cost of Dr. Osborne's care will be reimbursed through barter. While most patients make good on their trades, a few don't fulfill the full value; although this is disappointing to Dr. Osborne, she accepts it as part of the give-and-take of barter.

One delightful aspect of bartering is how it helps the Barter Clinic's employees. While Dr. Osborne's staff is paid in cash, they do receive bonuses in the form of bartered goods and services. That makes barter popular among her employees and keeps them motivated to give the best care possible.

patronizing the clinic and through the best advertising there is—word-of-mouth promotion. Reassure the clinician that you will be delighted to tell everyone you come in contact with about her excellent care. And the new patients she gains from you (and other barter patients) will lead to additional cash or insured patients.

Remind her that she is still getting value for her services; the currency is just being paid in whatever you will be offering for barter rather than cash. Better still, the office staff will spend less time processing your account than they would an insurance claim because it will essentially be handled as a cash transaction. No need to worry about extra forms, rejected claims from insurers, partial payments, co-pays that have to be collected, or advance approvals from insurers. When the office staff spend less time processing your files, they are more productive, which holds down overhead costs for the provider and frees staff time to deal with other issues, like getting reimbursed from other cases.

Depending on what you are offering to barter, you could further reduce overhead by eliminating some of their operating costs, such as paying a cleaning company or a temporary employee to answer phones when the receptionist is on vacation, or other services. The provider also ensures that your account doesn't wind up as bad debt, wasting staff time trying to hunt you down for payment.

Finally, remind her that your referrals could bring in cash-paying patients who pay more than insured patients and bring cash into the office faster than insurance payments do. It never hurts to remind the provider that since you have to work harder to set up the trade and make sure you meet your end of the deal, you are more motivated to follow the doctor's orders and more likely to have a better outcome. Health professionals prefer to care for patients who follow doctors' suggestions. Since you're more involved in the process than patients who just show up, flash their insurance cards, and do nothing to follow up, the provider will enjoy working with you more in both the short and the long run.

We suspect that if you are able to successfully educate the clinician, demonstrate the value of barter to her, and provide her with something she wants, you will be able to get the health care you need not only for yourself but also for your family—a proposition that can be a true lifesaver.

PAYING DOWN DEBTS

If you're like a lot of Americans, especially older ones, you're carrying medical debt from past care you didn't have insurance for or care that wasn't covered fully by insurance. Barter is a great way to try to reduce that debt. This is a great way to relieve a considerable strain on you and your family's finances, as well as make your clinician more willing to provide additional care for you or your family.

If you are too sick to barter, this is the time to ask family and friends to step into the gap for you and barter on your behalf. Rally your troops to help. In dire situations, people are often eager to help, especially when they don't have to dig into their own wallets to do so.

Here's a script to use when talking to a provider or office manager about paying down medical debts:

> *When I came to you, I had every intention of paying in cash. But with [insert situation here: the economy/ job loss/etc.], my circumstances have changed. I really want to honor that debt. Would you be open to barter, either directly or through an exchange, if you are a member of one? This would be a great*

way to get this off your receivables list and not have to write it off as bad debt or charity care.

With a bit of perseverance, you can get your caregiver to agree, and you'll be well on your way to paying off your debts and feeling the relief that will bring.

EXCHANGE-BASED TRADES

All of the previous trades have been based on direct barter, which always takes more effort to make a match than if you are working through a commercial trade exchange. If you want to jump on the medical superhighway, getting health care through a trade exchange will speed up the process dramatically. Before you approach a provider in the exchange, do the same type of investigating of that provider to make sure he or she is someone you'd want to deal with. Ask your broker for referrals to the providers who are members in the exchange. He or she will have a handle on whether other members have been satisfied by the care they have received and if they would trade with the clinician again.

If there are several providers of the same type of care, such as two or three dentists or general practitioner physicians, ask your broker which one other members have seemed the happiest with. We also recommend that you call the provider before making an appointment to check his or her prices. You may find that one dentist charges significantly more for the same service as another in the same exchange. Even in barter, you don't want to pay more for a service than you have to. Be an informed consumer and treat your medical trade just as you would in the cash world. You wouldn't go buy tires without asking what the price is; the same applies for health care.

For these trades, you'll have to set up the visit yourself and tell the appointment setter you are with a barter exchange. At the provider's office, you'll swipe your barter debit card or fill out a paper debit form to pay for the service you receive. Once you've done that, you're finished and on your way.

In most exchanges, you'll have no trouble finding certain providers, such as chiropractors and dentists. But for other professions, there won't be as many choices. If you need a specialist such as a plastic surgeon or anesthesiologist, you and your broker will have to try to recruit that particular type of specialist into the exchange. Just as in a direct trade, it helps if you are referred by another clinician when approaching the provider about becoming an exchange member. Your broker should be able to help you make the connections to bring the provider aboard.

If what you really want is health insurance, you'll be out of luck with a barter exchange. Insurers have such a lucrative cash business that they don't belong to exchanges, although there are certainly plenty of exchange owners who would love to recruit them. By the same token, you'll have difficulty bartering with particular hospitals and highly paid specialists, such as surgeons whose care relies on many others. While you might be able to barter for just the surgeon's fees, you will still be looking at a cash bill for all the medical equipment, nursing care, time in the operating room, X-rays, diagnostic testing, and other medical services provided by the hospital as part of the surgery.

While barter can certainly help, the complicated nature of the medical system makes trading a much more difficult proposition for the full range of services that people need. If you aren't in an emergency situation, and you've got some time before the care is given, you can try to set up as many trades as possible in advance. You may even be in a better bargaining position with the health-care firm or provider once care has been rendered and once they understand that you don't have much cash for paying medical bills. Just remember: It never hurts to introduce the idea of barter into a situation. You might be pleasantly surprised at what emerges from the discussion.

INTERNET SITES

Probably the most popular way to try to find health care through barter is through Web sites like U-Exchange, CraigsList, and Favorpals. Most often, people are seeking dental care or general medical care. Others are looking for plastic surgery and vision services—typically the types of care that aren't covered by basic health insurance plans.

Of course we support barter over the Internet and encourage you to try out these sites and others. But you may find that making a match is especially slow going when it comes to health care. For that reason, you might be better served by contacting a medical provider yourself and trying to initiate a direct trade. That's especially true if you have an urgent medical need. Some health-care trades can take months over Web sites, in part because the most in-demand providers have plenty of cash business coming their way and don't feel the desire to barter. When you add to that the reluctance of many health-care professionals to engage in barter because they don't understand it, have never heard of it, or think it might be unethical, you can see why the pool of available traders is small.

But here are some tips that could help you speed up the process and make a great trade. Be very specific and general at the same time when you are listing what you have to offer and what you want. Sounds like we're speaking in opposites, right? But here's what we mean: When you list what the service is you want, be as specific as possible so the provider knows if he or she is potentially a good match for you. Instead of listing "Dental care needed," say "Root canal needed." With the latter example, you'll be alerting general dentists who don't do root canals that you aren't a good prospect for them. You are really looking for endodontists or general dentists who *do* offer this procedure.

The same applies for the "offering" column of the Web site. Be specific about what you can offer in trade—even if it sounds corny. You never know. Just like the general population, health-care providers have a varied list of interests. Doctors who live in the suburbs often have fireplaces and could use a cord of wood. Dentists who live in the inner city like to go hunting and could use a shotgun. Perhaps the chiropractor on the Web site has been yearning for years to learn to play the banjo, and it's possible that the physical therapist would like to have fresh-baked bread from your oven every week. And who can't use a massage or maybe a side of beef? Remember that people in professions often don't have basic skills like drywalling, carpentry, or gardening. They often lack vehicles or equipment that you might have available, like a truck to haul the internist's college student daughter and all her stuff to school, a rototiller to turn the speech therapist's garden, or a ceramic tile cutter to replace the damaged tile in the optometrist's office. Include the most enticing services or goods you have available in the headline of your Web site listing, but don't stop there. Continue your list of available trades within the body of the listing. Cover as much ground as you can, and at the end of your listing, say that you're open to other ideas.

Also be mindful of the other goods and services that your extended family and friends might be able to offer on your behalf. If your daughter needs to see a specialist, we bet you have several friends who could offer their van for moving, lessons on a musical instrument, or lawn-care work for trade just to help you and your little one get the care she needs. You can trade your friend something in return and make it a three-way trade. This is about creativity and finding out what each person wants and needs.

Another tip is to repost your need from time to time and reshuffle what you have to offer. If your offer of firewood or honey didn't attract any takers, change your headline items to something else from your longer list. Or if you've managed to find a friend who will trade on your behalf, or as a three-way trade, list the friend's good or service in your headline.

Actively search for providers yourself in the Web site's member profiles. Don't limit yourself to professionals located only in your town, particularly if you need a specialist. Normally you might not want to drive fifty miles to see an ophthalmologist, but if you have vision problems and you find one who will barter with you, it makes the money you spent on gasoline well worth the trip.

Make sure you don't post on just one site. While sites like Favorpals have a special barter section dedicated to health care alone, general trading sites still have plenty of professionals trolling their pages. Put the need out on as many sites as possible. Search the older listings for professionals who listed their services thirty or sixty days ago or even further in the past. If someone has traded once, he might be willing to trade again, especially if the previous trade was satisfying.

Another tactic is to send messages to the people who posted a need for the same type of care you desire. Ask them if they were able to make a trade. If they did, ask who the clinician was who bartered with them and if the trade went well on both sides in their opinion. (If it didn't, you probably will not want to contact that provider, either because of substandard care or because the trade went poorly, and the well is now poisoned for additional trades because of that one bad experience.) Contact that person directly. Make sure you get the patient's name before you call, or write the professional so you've got a referral to offer rather than just calling cold.

Ultimately, Web site health-care trades take more patience and persistence than direct trades. But the time and energy you spend will be worthwhile to get the care you need.

TIME BANKS

For people who have time that they would like to trade for health care, time banks can be their rescuers. A time bank, unlike a trade exchange, is often a social justice effort designed to alleviate poverty by giving people who join the time bank access to services (and sometimes goods) that they couldn't otherwise afford in exchange for their services. Members of the bank earn scrip (or currency) called "time dollars" for every hour of service they provide for another member. Their time can be earned by giving highly valuable services such as plumbing, electrical, accounting, or home repair. But members also earn time dollars from typically lower-cost or uncompensated services, such as driving a member to the doctor, going to see a movie with another member, or taking a pet for a walk.

In some cases, the members who earn time dollars are in poor health, and they are assisting another member who is in even poorer health. The rewards, especially for seniors, are immense. For a generation that prides itself on refusing charity and relying on self-sufficiency, barter through time dollars is an acceptable means of enriching their lives and ensuring that they stay vital and, in some cases, in their own homes rather than at a nursing facility. Helping another person in some way, no matter how small, is a great way to feel vibrant and good about yourself.

In some cities, time banks also exist for health-care services. They are rarities, but they do exist. Sometimes they are referred to as a health-care cooperative, or the time bank could be a single hospital or clinic that barters with patients and their families for time worked at the facility in payment of their bill. Often this refers to patients who are able to work in the clinic or doctor's office that provides the care. You don't need to be a nurse or an X-ray technician to do the work. It could be as simple as answering phones, filing papers, or cleaning the office. Even doctors who work for time-bank clinics receive far less for their services than if they were paid in cash. They do it out of a desire to care for people who desperately need treatment but have no money for health insurance or office visits. In other cases, the time dollars are earned by providing babysitting for another member who needs to be seen by a clinician, driving an elder to an office appointment or pharmacy, or, in the instance of a member who is homebound, calling another member to check in and make sure all is well.

To make this system work, the normally highly paid doctors and nurses who work at the health-care cooperative, like the one in Ithaca, New York (see Ithaca Hours program, mentioned in "Time Banks," chapter 4), or stand-alone clinics like Family Health Care in Kansas City, Kansas, accept much lower pay than they would normally require. For instance, at the clinic in Kansas City, physicians are paid as little as $11 an hour. Patients are often asked to pay in a combination of time barter and cash, based on a sliding scale adjusted to their income level. While these sorts of co-ops and clinics aren't numerous, you can determine if there is one near you by searching the Internet, as well as going to www.timebanks.org.

GET CREATIVE

While setting up direct trades and using Web sites or barter exchanges are wonderful avenues for getting the health care you need, we also encourage you to strap on your thinking cap and dream up a creative way to use barter to get care. We especially like the tack taken by Antonio Puri, a painter in Westchester, Pennsylvania. Many professional artists lack health insurance because they are self-employed. Artists often take a double hit when the economy goes through a recession and fewer people have the money to buy their artwork. One day, Puri was watching his three-year-old son trading Pokémon cards with a buddy, and an idea struck him: Why not hold an art show offering the artwork for barter instead of cash?

In short order, Puri had gathered a group of fellow artists and organized Art4Barter, a gallery exhibit in which the artists determine what they will accept in trade for their creations. Many of the artists listed health-care services as their desired item. Painter Paul Santoleri traded his work for a doctor's care and medications. Puri himself was able to trade one of his paintings with a dentist, who provided a root canal and a crown.

How could you apply that sort of creativity to your own health-care needs? Here are a few ideas to try or to spark your own imagination:

- If you are a hairstylist, organize a Beauty4Barter event and let patrons bid on haircuts, color, braiding, facials, waxing, or any other service you and your colleagues can provide.
- If you can provide lawn care and have a cadre of landscapers who are the best darned flower planters, ornamental pond installers, or tree trimmers around, host a Dig4Barter event.
- Musicians are one of the many professionals who don't typically have health insurance. Band together and offer a smorgasbord of different services. How about Music4Barter? Musicians could offer to compose a special

song for a sweetheart, play your daughter's bat mitzvah or the company picnic, dedicate their next album to your wife, or play a benefit concert for your favorite charity.

- This doesn't have to be just for creative folk either. Are you a geek? Get your geek squad together and offer a computer clinic as Geeks4Barter where people can bid on having you and your buddies debug, upgrade, pimp out, or rev up traders' machines.

Apply a little creativity to the situation, get your colleagues or friends involved, promote the heck out of, and, most of all, have a ball. You could find your next great doctor, chiropractor, or acupuncturist in the bargain.

GREAT TRADE!

When artist Maria Nevelson decided to include her sculpture #04.7.1 *Mandarava of the Marsh* in the Art4Barter gallery exhibition in Philadelphia, Pennsylvania, she was allowed to list three "payments" she would accept for the piece. After chatting about it with a friend over drinks, she decided to list her payments as

1) A husband
2) $6,200
3) Dental work

Since she was forty-nine and had never been married, it just seemed like good fun to list a husband as the first payment. She also figured she should be practical and list the dental work, since she needed it. And besides, *Mandarava of the Marsh* was the largest sculpture she had ever created, and she wasn't in a rush to sell it.

The night of the exhibition opening, other artists were listing interesting items they wanted for their artwork, such as a unisex bicycle, matting services, and software for the blind. But when people saw Maria's asking price, they burst out laughing. Maria had great fun with the whole experiment and chalked it up to a good time.

During the show, a man put his name and phone number down next to the "husband" option on her offer sheet. He told her he would like to apply for boyfriend status by taking her out on a date. Startled and embarrassed at the same time, she agreed to go out with him to discuss his trade more fully, and without nearly everyone in the gallery watching and listening.

After their first date a week later, Maria called the gallery and instructed the staff to mark *Mandarava of the Marsh* as OFFER ACCEPTED—which is just too perfect, since the Buddhist goddess Mandarava, as the story goes, fled from her father when he tried to stop her from marrying her guru. After she and her guru survive her father's attempt to burn them in a pyre, she becomes her guru's consort and a venerated deity of wisdom. Mandarava is, Maria notes, the goddess Buddhists pray to for help in removing obstacles in life.

TRADING TIP

If you haven't been to a doctor in years, ask a family member who has for a referral. Mention that you're Uncle Joe's youngest niece when you call to talk to the doctor about bartering. The doctor will want to keep Uncle Joe's business, so you'll have a better shot at making a trade.

TRADING TIP

If you're drowning in medical debt, check to see if there is a time bank in your town. If there is, the doctor or hospital that you owe may allow you to earn time dollars to pay off your debts.

RESOURCES

GENERAL BARTER INFORMATION

Check out BarterStrategies.com for general information about all aspects of barter.

BARTER OR TRADE SITES

AssetFair.com for trading luxury or high-priced items or debts
BarterBart.com for general trading
Barterfest.net for general barter and auctions
BarterPalace.com for general trading
BarterQuest.com for general barter
BarterSwitch.com for general barter
CareToTrade.com for general and real estate trade (in beta
   test version)

CraigsList.org has a general bartering section for many cities

Favorpals.com for general barter and health care

GoSwap.com for vehicles and real estate

SwapAce.com for general trades, free items, and sales

SwapatHome.com for general trading with coupons as a form of scrip

SwapGiant.com for general trading

Swap-It-Now.com for general trading

Swap.net for general trading with scrip (membership fee)

SwapTreasures.com for general trades

TradeAFavor.com, a Facebook.com-based site for general trade

TradeAmericaOnline.com for general barter in the U.S.

TradeAway.com for trading vehicles and general items (allows auctions and cash sales)

TradeGlobalOnline.com for general barter outside the U.S.

TradeYaInc.com for general barter (with a membership and transaction fees

Trashbank.com for general barter and cash sales

U-Exchange.com is a general barter site for goods, services, and residential real estate

USwapIt.com for general trading

GRASSROOTS / DIRECT EXCHANGES / BARTER CLUBS

antoniopuri.com/Art4Barter.htm, the site for Art4Barter (paintings, sculpture, photography, and other art available through barter)

Barter4Kids.com is the Web site for the barter clothing exchange in Willow Spring, North Carolina

FloridaBarterBanque.com, located in mid-Florida, for business and individual barter

Grace Hill Settlement House has a time bank at www.
gracehill.org

Hubbell Trading Post is a working U.S. government–run
trading post for Native American goods that accepts
barter (nps.gov/hutr/index.htm)

IthacaHours.org is the site for the barter system set up in
Ithaca, New York

MadisonHours.org is a time bank in Madison, Wisconsin

Meetup.com is a searchable Web site with barter groups as
well as other community groups that might have barter
activities

Michigan Barter Marketplace (www.mibartermarketplace.
com)

musee-solomon.com, for the artist Pablo Solomon, who
trades his paintings, drawings, and sculpture

PaulGlover.org, for information about starting a community
barter system such as the one Paul Glover started in
Ithaca, New York

St. Louis Barter (StLouisBarter.com)

TimeBanks.org for information about starting and managing
a time-bank barter system

HOME OR VACATION BARTER SITES

AllStates1031.com is an intermediary that handles barter real
estate exchanges for clients nationwide

DomuSwap.com for trading real estate

ExchangeHomes.com for permanent trades

Federation of Exchange Accommodators, www.1031.org, or
(215) 564-3484 (maintains a list of firms that can assist
with 1031 barter property transactions)

4homex.com for global home exchanges

GoSwap.org for real estate trades

HomeBase-hols.com for holiday trades

HomeExchange.com for swapping homes on vacation
HomeLink.org for swapping homes on vacation
OnlineHouseTrading.com for real estate trades
RealEstateExchange.com for real estate trades

NATIONAL/INTERNATIONAL TRADE ASSOCIATIONS

IRTA.org is the International Reciprocal Trade Association
NATE.org is the National Association of Trade Exchanges

BARTER EXCHANGE CHAINS OR FRANCHISORS

International Monetary Systems (imsbarter.com)
ITEX (itex.com)

SPECIALTY BARTER

BookMooch.com for books
Bookswap.com for textbooks
CellSwapper.com to trade your cell phone
CellTradeUSA.com to trade your cell phone contract
Favorpals.com for general barter and health-care trades
Kidzoodle.com for trading and auctioning children's items
PaperbackSwap.com for books
Points.com to swap frequent flier miles from one airline to
    another
Rehashclothes.com for clothing, accessories, and books
SwapALease.com for trading your car's lease for another
    lease
Swapnstuff.com for trading DVDs, CDs, books, textbooks,
    and video games to earn points
SwapTree.com for books, movies, CDs, and games

TheSwap.com for homeschool curriculum materials
TotsSwapShop.com for children's items
ToySwap.com
ToysToTrade.com
VeggieTrader.com to buy, sell, or trade produce

CLOTHING TRADES

ChicagoClothingSwap.wordpress.com
ClothingSwaps.com
DigNSwap.com
SwapStyle.com

BABYSITTING CO-OPS

BabySittingCoop.com to learn more about how to set up
    your own co-op
BabysitterExchange.com to learn more about how to set up
    your own co-op
HelpingHero.com to purchase software to calculate points
    in a co-op

GIFT CARDS EXCHANGES

CardAvenue.com
PlasticJungle.com
SwapAGift.com
TheGiftCardTrader.com

FLEA MARKETS / SWAP MEETS

BlossomSwap.com for trading plants and bulbs
Classic Bicycle Swap meet in Ann Arbor, Michigan, at
    ann-arbor-bicycleshow.com

Craftster.org to organize swap meets of craft projects
ListingFleaMarket.com
Swap.bead-patterns.com for trading beads
Swap-bot.com lets users organize their own swap meets
Swap Meet in Riverdale, Utah, at motorvu.com

BARTER CONTRACTS

Docstoc.com has a downloadable barter contract that
can be used at no cost at http://www.docstoc.com/
docs/2836850/barter-agreement

MONEY VERSUS BARTER LESSON PLAN

Grade Level 2nd Grade   Length of Lesson 50 minutes

I. Prior Knowledge

To assess the students' prior knowledge, have students
complete a crossword puzzle. The crossword puzzle assesses
the students' understanding of the economic vocabulary
words. The across and the down columns give the students
the definition of the vocabulary words. The students' vocabulary words or answers will be in a key box. The students
will figure out which economic vocabulary word fits with
the correct definition. This activity allows the students to
review the economic vocabulary words that will be discussed
throughout the unit.

II. Goal

To explain or demonstrate how people trade and barter.

III. Learner Outcomes

Before the group discussion, the students will complete
an economic vocabulary crossword puzzle with 75 percent
accuracy. (Knowledge & Comprehension)

During a whole class activity, the students will participate in a game of trade and bartering with no errors. (Application)

After the whole class activity, the students will complete a poster that will name what they were able to barter or trade, with 80 percent accuracy. (Application)

During an individual activity, the students will complete a worksheet and explain any difficulties they had with trading. The goal is 80 percent accuracy. (Evaluation)

IV. Procedures

A. Preassessment/Vocabulary crossword puzzle (Intrapersonal, Linguistic, Logical)

1. Before the lesson, hand the students a vocabulary crossword puzzle to complete.

2. Differentiation: Allow the students to work in teams of two. This will allow students to work together to figure out the answers. Students who are stronger in reading can work with those who struggle with reading and vocabulary.

3. This vocabulary crossword puzzle will assess the students' understanding of the economic vocabulary words to be discussed throughout the unit. They include *barter, trade, money, cash, exchange, buy, sell, value, goods, services, currency, scrip, wants, needs,* and *fairness.*

4. Give the students ample time to complete the preassessment.

B. Read aloud *The Ox-Cart Man*/book discussion (Interpersonal, Linguistic, Spatial)

1. Begin the book by asking a question.

   a. "Have you ever made anything to sell?" (Knowledge)

2. After the book is finished, ask the students a series of questions.

    a. "What were some of the things the man and his family made?" (Comprehension)

    b. "What were some of the things the man and his family grew or collected?" (Comprehension)

    c. "What other items did the farmer sell?" (Comprehension)

    d. "What did the farmer get at the market in Portsmouth?" (Comprehension)

4. Write all their answers on a whiteboard so the students will be able to reflect on them later on throughout the lesson.

C. Discuss economic concepts: natural resources, exchange, and barter (Linguistic, Interpersonal, Logical, Spatial)

    1. Explain what natural resources are to the class.

    2. Make a list of the natural resources from the book.

    3. Explain what trade, barter, and exchange are.

    4. Explain the new vocabulary by telling the students stories.

        a. "Almost everyone has traded something at some time. If you brought a peanut butter and jelly sandwich for lunch, but you're tired of peanut butter and jelly, you might trade for your friend's turkey and cheese sandwich."

        b. "What are some other things people sometimes trade for?" (Analysis)

        c. "When you trade for something else, we say you have *exchanged* these items. Do you remember the word *exchange*?" (Knowledge)

        d. "One way to exchange things is to barter them. A long time ago, before money was invented, people would use barter to get the things they needed that they couldn't get for themselves. One person might

have loved to fish. He fished all day long. He had
lots and lots of fish, but he really wanted some milk
and cheese items, although he didn't have a cow."

    e. "How could he get milk or butter or cheese?" (Analysis)

    f. "The man with the fish could find a man with a cow
and barter with him."

    g. "What do you think they might exchange?"
(Synthesis)

D. Large group activity: Trading and bartering game (Interpersonal, Spatial, Linguistic, Logical, Bodily-Kinetics)

    1. Group four to five students into separate "countries"
that will be bartering.

    2. Appoint a leader of each country.

    3. Have students cut and paste their flag onto the country's poster.

    4. Each student will then write the name of their country
and the names of their fellow citizens.

    5. Each student will pick one item they would like to
have for their country.

    6. Each student will list the item obtained on one side
of the poster, labeled SELL.

    7. The students will then work with their team to decide
what they would like to barter and trade for with the
other countries.

    8. Remind them that they should pick items that would
be beneficial for survival, that is, yarn (clothing),
bread (food), tea (beverage), wood (shelter).

    9. Allow ten minutes or so for trading.

    10. Students will list each item they bartered for on the
other side of the poster, labeled BOUGHT.

E. Individual activity/The Trouble with Trading worksheet (Intrapersonal, Linguistic, Logical)

1. Explain the individual activity to the students.

2. Hand out a worksheet to the students that asks the following questions: Did you have enough items to trade to get everything you wanted? Were some items more popular than others? Did you have trouble getting people to trade with you at times? Why? Were some items more valuable than others? Why? Why is barter harder to use than money?

3. Allow plenty of time for students to finish the worksheet.

F. Closure-sharing (Interpersonal, Linguistic)

After this activity, the students will be given time to share and to talk about the difference between bartering (or trading) and money.

Lesson plan provided by elementary educator Tara Stitzel of St. Louis, Missouri.

Sample Barter Agreement

Date: [   ]

Name: [   ]

Phone: [   ]   E-mail: [   ]

Address: [   ]

[   ]

City: [   ]   State: [   ]   Zip code: [   ]

Is bartering/trading for:

Describe product or services (be descriptive and spell out terms):

[   ]

[   ]

[   ]

To:

Name: [   ]

Phone: [   ]   E-mail: [   ]

Address: [   ]

[   ]

City: [   ]   State: [   ]   Zip code: [   ]

Is bartering/trading for:

Describe product or services (be descriptive and spell out terms):

[   ]

[   ]

[   ]

Neither party is paying cash, as this is a barter transaction.

Signed: [   ]   Date: [   ]

Signed: [   ]   Date: [   ]

Trade Tracking

Date	Product/ Service Traded	Product/ Service Received	Traded with Name	Phone Number	Value

Sample Trade Purchase Request

For Barter Exchange Member

Product or service needed:

Current vendor _____ Current volume: _____

Is this a _____one-time or _____ ongoing need?
(Please check one)

Approximate cost if one-time: _____

Approximate cost per month if ongoing: _____

Best-qualified supplier:

Company name: _____

Web site: _____

Contact: _____

Phone number: _____

Second-best-qualified supplier:

Company name: _____

Web site: _____

Contact: _____

Phone number: _____

Third-best-qualified supplier:

Company name: _____

Web site: _____

Contact: _____

Phone number: _____

Also Available from **SKYHORSE PUBLISHING**

10,001 Ways to Live Large on a Small Budget

You can have the good life, even in bad times!

$14.95 paperback

The Joy of Keeping Chickens

Use your backyard to produce meat and eggs.

$14.95 paperback

Back to Basics

Growing your own, household skills, and more.

$24.95 hardcover

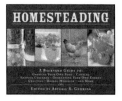

Homesteading

Herbs, crafts, gardening, and more.

$24.95 hardcover

Odd Jobs

Earn extra money any time any place—for students, retirees, or anyone tired of the old nine to five.

$12.95 paperback

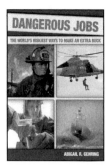

Dangerous Jobs

Fun and fabulous full- and part-time jobs for adrenaline junkies.

$12.95 paperback

Preserving

Make the most of what you grow, save money and eat healthier.

$12.95 hardcover

Home Brewing

Brew at home for the perfect beer for any occasion.

$12.95 hardcover